Finalist for the
2019 BANFF MOUNTAIN BOOK
COMPETITION AWARD *in*
ADVENTURE TRAVEL, *the*
WILLIAM HILL SPORTS BOOK
of the YEAR AWARD, *and the*
STEPPES TRAVEL ADVENTURE
TRAVEL BOOK *of the* YEAR AWARD

a BUZZFEED BOOK CLUB
OFFICIAL PICK

———————————————

"An inspirational tale of struggle—dehydration, injury and
isolation—ultimately overcome through grit and sheer willpower."
—*The Wall Street Journal Magazine*

"Prior-Palmer writes with a dash and boldness
few writers possess . . . Remarkable."
—NPR

"The book's emotional impact lies in the nuanced
portrait of its subject searching
for answers beyond the life she's lived so far."
—*Entertainment Weekly*

NATIONAL BESTSELLER

Praise for *Rough Magic*

Named a Best Book of the Year by *The Daily Mail*, *Esquire*, *Electric Literature*, and *Literary Hub*

Finalist for the 2019 Banff Mountain Book Competition Award in Adventure Travel, the William Hill Sports Book of the Year Award, and the Steppes Travel Adventure Travel Book of the Year Award

A BuzzFeed Book Club Official Pick

"If you like your memoirs to revolve around singular experiences, Lara Prior-Palmer's *Rough Magic* delivers." —JOHN WILLIAMS, *The New York Times*

"An inspirational tale of struggle—dehydration, injury and isolation—ultimately overcome through grit and sheer willpower."
—THOMAS GEBREMEDHIN, *The Wall Street Journal Magazine*

"This is no fresh-forged mythic hero, but rather a young woman who's still doubting, still equivocating about her right to seek greatness . . . To her credit, the heroine of this story never claims to be flawless, nor even to be a heroine. Ultimately, the book lingers in the mind partly for its fearless prose and partly for its refusal to obey that tired old victorious arc of the journey narrative. Prior-Palmer both embraces the race and disavows it. She pulls back to observe the minutiae of the moment, the marmot holes that riddle the steppe and the infinite, individual blades of grass that paint it green. She offers no easy morals on these dual modes of life and of narrative . . . As Prior-Palmer senses on her journey, reconciling the wisdom of the everyday with the instinct for timelessness and mythmaking is a life's work—work to which *Rough Magic* is an engaging guide." —ELLIE ROBBINS, *The Washington Post*

"Excellent prose and rigorous honesty . . . An unusual pleasure to read . . . Prior-Palmer writes with a dash and boldness few writers possess; her language seems sui generis . . . Her narrative alchemy is remarkable; in every chapter, she turns boredom to suspense and back again. The Derby is at once heart-stoppingly close and a miserable slog to which we already know the ending. That shifting—heroism to comedy, glamour to stinking holes in the ground—creates a tension far more interesting than the question of who's going to win the race, or how."   —LILY MEYER, NPR

"The author's prose is poetic, and while the race and Mongolian landscape are conjured beautifully and intensely, the book's emotional impact lies in the nuanced portrait of its subject searching for answers beyond the life she's lived so far."   —DAVID CANFIELD, *Entertainment Weekly*

"Think the next *Educated* or *Wild*. Palmer's memoir of beating the odds to become a horse champion is an inspiring saga of perseverance—and a classic underdog tale."   —*Entertainment Weekly*, 1 of the 15 Most Anticipated Books of the Year

"What unfolds, Cheryl Strayed–like, is her thrilling gallop to the finish line."   —*O, The Oprah Magazine*, One of the Best Books by Women of the Season

"*Rough Magic* succeeds on its realness and Prior-Palmer's unsparing analysis of herself and the scene . . . Even in the down moments, when one of her ponies is temporarily injured and she's struggling, the fast-paced book is lyrical and full of tight, action-packed sentences. It reads like it came bursting out of her."   —HEATHER HANSMAN, *Outside*

"Taking off on a horse into the Mongolian Steppe sounds like the bracing inverse to an overpopulated, busy urban life, but having the skills and grit to pull it off is another thing entirely. Lara Prior-Palmer attempted the Mongol Derby not really knowing what she was getting into; she ended it knowing much more about herself, and a race champion besides."   —ESTELLE TANG, *Elle*

"It feels so tired to call a book inspiring, but that's exactly what *Rough Magic* is . . . Thanks to Lara's uncanny ability to make the reader feel like they're in this race with her, you'll be captivated from start to finish—and find yourself missing the book when it's over." —MEHERA BONNER, *Cosmopolitan*

"Forthright and exhilarating . . . A frank and delightful blend of extreme sports and travel writing." —ERIN KEANE, *Salon*

"An instant classic memoir . . . With whip-smart sass and achingly beautiful observations on life, Prior-Palmer easily breaks us in as she canters across the wild verdant steppes of Mongolia, where the vastness is matched only by the author's unbridled spirit of adventure. We're reminded that despite battling bone-deep fatigue in sweat-soaked clothes, we too have what it takes to stay upright—no matter how many times we may get knocked down." —LAUREN MATISON, *Shape*

"Forthcoming, perceptive and humorous . . . Prior-Palmer's account of her race across the Mongolian steppe is consistently joyful. It reminds us that joy can encompass chronic stomach pain, jammed thumbs, soaked jodhpurs, lost maps, angry boys throwing stones and the brutal tedium of 1,000 kilometers on horseback . . . Her gleeful words alone are worth the ride." —MORGAN HUNTER THOMAS, *Ms.*

"First-time author Prior-Palmer transforms from hopeless 19-year-old underdog into surprising champion of the grueling 2013 Mongol Derby in this exhilarating, visceral account of her attempt to win a 1,000-kilometer horse race across the Mongolian countryside . . . Filled with soulful self-reflection and race detail, this fast-paced page-turner is a thrill ride from start to finish." —*Publishers Weekly* (starred review)

"Page by page, Prior-Palmer tunes us in, slows us down to her speed, to pony paces, and we begin to attend to the present moment just as she does . . . At every turn, Prior-Palmer's writing is brilliant and clear-eyed and demonstrates more wisdom than any philosopher's theories." —ABBY TRAVIS, *San Francisco Chronicle*

"An astonishing and hair-raising memoir that you, too, will race to finish."

—*Newsweek*

"In this sensual, spiritual memoir, Prior-Palmer recounts her grueling journey through immense physical hardship, and her surprising transformation from underdog to champion."

—ADRIENNE WESTENFELD, *Esquire*,
One of the Best Books to Read This Season

"Absolutely riveting."

—*BuzzFeed*

"[Prior-Palmer's] gorgeous, sensual depiction of this race is a literary marvel; it feels like you are riding alongside her across the desolate steppes; her verbal acuity makes vivid the most elusive of landscapes; her triumph becomes ours."

—KRISTIN IVERSEN, *NYLON*

"An awesome (like literally awesome) memoir of how Prior-Palmer became the youngest person to finish, not to mention the first woman to win 'the world's longest, toughest horse race.' That would be the ten-day Mongol Derby, which is organized based on the messenger system used by Genghis Khan. So, no big deal or anything."

—EMILY TEMPLE, *Literary Hub*

"[A] stirring new memoir . . . Many, many readers are going to be charmed by *Rough Magic*, whether they can tack up a horse or not, and rightly so. The setting is exotic. The challenge is extreme. The protagonist is winsome and imperfect . . . The magnitude of what she ultimately achieves 'stun[s] her into writing,' but it's not healing that Prior-Palmer seeks, or even liberation. It's the 'world in the raw,' something many of us have learned to crave."

—ALYSON HAGY, *Literary Hub*

"The narrator's peculiar syntax, unabashed youth, and victory against a hell of a lot of odds kept the book in my happy hands."

—COURTNEY MAUM, *The Rumpus*

"From the opening pages of *Rough Magic*, readers understand they are entering the mind of a unique personality . . . Prior-Palmer describes the Mongol Derby as 'a perfect hodgepodge of Snakes and Ladders and the Tour de France on unknown bicycles.' As a former horseback rider with an adventurous streak (who also happens to appreciate the Tour de France), I was predisposed to enjoy this book. But it was turns of phrases like that, I quickly realized—surprising, playful, unexpected—that were going to make me love it." —HALIMAH MARCUS, *Electric Literature*

"Feisty and exhilarating . . . Horse lovers will adore this inspiring and spirited memoir." —*Kirkus Reviews*

"Palmer writes with grace, giving a measured, reflective account of the race she was unprepared for but still won, the rivalries and partnerships that sprung up between the competitors, and the ruggedly lovely, lonely landscape she traversed. An engaging profile of humans and horses, and a searing, soulful examination of endurance." —*Booklist*

"Few readers are more horse-crazy than teens, and Prior-Palmer's youthful perspective will speak to them." —*Booklist* (YA)

"A fresh, irreverent voice and a quick wit . . . It's a story worthy of the best adventure writers, and Prior-Palmer does not disappoint. An appealing account that will capture the imagination of a wide audience, including young adults. Readers who enjoyed Cheryl Strayed's *Wild* and James Campbell's *Braving It* will want to join Prior-Palmer on her once-in-a-lifetime trek." —*Library Journal*

"[Prior-Palmer's] visceral descriptions of each leg of the journey, and the unrelenting urge to defeat the frontrunner from Texas, make for an unforgettable story." —JANE CIABATTARI, BBC Culture, 1 of 10 Books to Read This Month

"Prior-Palmer already shares many qualities with classic English travel writers such as Rebecca West and Gertrude Bell, but she is also refreshingly self-aware . . . A heroic tale beautifully told." —CAROLINE EDEN, *The Times Literary Supplement*

"Prior-Palmer's style is a fascinating mix of pep and poignancy. A really terrific story by a spirited new voice." —SARA BAUME, author of *A Line Made by Walking*

"*Rough Magic* is the most entertaining memoir I've read in years. It's thrilling, hilarious, unexpected, and ultimately breathtaking. I loved every minute of this wild ride." —ABBY GENI, author of *The Wildlands*

"This debut memoir is a brilliant literary exploration of loneliness and an exhilarating, funny, soulful account of how one young woman, against all odds, won a truly extraordinary race." —KRISTEN RADTKE, author of *Imagine Wanting Only This*

"As fast-paced as the swiftest Mongolian racehorse, Lara Prior-Palmer's searingly honest account of her astonishing rise from hopeless underdog to Mongol Derby champion leaves grit in your teeth and dust in your hair. I laughed, I cried, and I felt every bruise. I was riveted until the last word and left with lasting daydreams of Mongolian horizons." —FELICITY ASTON, author of *Alone in Antarctica: The First Woman to Ski Solo Across the Southern Ice*

"Lara Prior-Palmer's writing collapses geological time into the velocity of the present instant, near and distant histories thrumming in the thoughts that beat between hoof-falls. In *Rough Magic* she possesses Annie Dillard's brilliance for noticing, laced with a wild and glistering humor. If an intellect can be said to be elemental, this is it." —JOSEPHINE ROWE, author of *A Loving, Faithful Animal*

"*Rough Magic* brims with urgency, wit, and insight. Lara Prior-Palmer is an author to remember, and she's written a book that wild horses couldn't drag me away from." —LILY BROOKS-DALTON, author of *Motorcycles I've Loved*

"*Rough Magic* is so charming, weird, and absorbing. I was fascinated by the race, and the utterly unique Prior-Palmer herself." —SOFIJA STEFANOVIC, author of *Miss Ex-Yugoslavia*

ROUGH MAGIC

Riding the World's Loneliest Horse Race

LARA PRIOR-PALMER

Catapult  New York

This book is a memoir. It reflects the author's
recollections of experiences over time.

Cover design by Nicole Caputo
Book design by Wah-Ming Chang

Hardcover ISBN: 978-1-948226-19-6
Paperback ISBN: 978-1-948226-98-1

Catapult titles are distributed to the trade
by Publishers Group West
Phone: 866-400-5351

Library of Congress Control Number: 2018950159

Printed in the United States of America
1 3 5 7 9 10 8 6 4 2

To Alfie

But this rough magic
I here abjure, and when I have required
Some heavenly music, which even now I do,
To work mine end upon their senses that
This airy charm is for, I'll break my staff,
Bury it certain fathoms in the earth,
And deeper than did ever plummet sound
I'll drown my book.

—*The Tempest*

ROUGH MAGIC

I

It was May 2013 when I was cooped up in an attic in Austria, au pairing for a family with six Ferraris. They lived in a converted hotel in the jaws of an Alpine valley.

"Lara? Larah!"

Every morning the mother shrieked my name up the endless floors. "Time to feed the baby!"

I had taken the role to practice my German, but she only spoke in English. My jobs varied from sitting with the toddler to vacuuming up the dead skin that snowed from his father's bottom.

The family never left their house except to get in their cars, which they kept tucked up in the garage. They viewed their valley through window frames as you would a photograph. So sedentary a lifestyle in such physical surroundings made me itch. At night I hatched plans to creep up the mountain and slide down the other side into Switzerland, yet the mother looked appalled when I so much as suggested running to the church and back.

By the time she sacked me a month later, my body was rusty and yearning for usage. I returned to the silent butterflies of an England on the brink of summer, seeking an experience unlike any I'd had before. In theory, this ought not to have been difficult. The most exciting moment in my eighteen years had been collecting chickens from Dorset on the train and wrapping them up in wine crates for Christmas presents.

The next month, June, marked a year since my release from high school. Fleeing the red bricks had been my dream for years—at fourteen, I had thought of myself as the finished article, ready to either have babies or break free (to where I couldn't say, though for many years I had been fixated on becoming a burglar). Despite my conviction that more education would poison me like pesticide on a lush forest, I had remained in London until I passed my final exams. Strangely, the dissolution of structure thereafter unnerved me.

What was it about turning into an adult? The color drained from the days and life became a calendar. I floated in a debris of possible dates and implausible plans, with neither the funding nor the fervor to propel me onwards. Friends were busy with jobs or university, inclined to holiday on beaches rather than accompany me to Kyrgyzstan—a place I fantasized about. Meanwhile, I hadn't heard back from my application to go organic farming in Wales, nor from the orphanage placement in Ethiopia. Dead-end jobs and equestrian competitions came and went. I moved through the month of my birthday without any fixed direction.

It was a warm city day when, for the umpteenth time, I cast my rod into the depths of Google as if the internet might contain my future. After opening and abandoning endless tabs, I brought up the page of a horse race.

The passing London Underground train shook the building as I leaned into the photograph—long-maned ponies streaming over green steppes, space poured wide and free—in *Mongolia*. The open-voweled sounds of the word matched the freedom the country conjured in my mind. I couldn't place Mongolia in history, nor could I place it on the map. The magnolia tree outside the window had passed full bloom; its pink petals were turning brown on the pavement. For a while my head merged these two words— Mongolia, magnolia; Mongolia, magnolia.

I had spotted the Mongol Derby online many years before, but the entry fee was exorbitant (around $6,000 at the time) and I knew I'd never afford it, at least not until I was towing some dull job along in my thirties. Sadly, the price was now even higher, thirty riders were already signed on, and the entry deadline for the August race had passed. I moved the mouse to quit the page, blinking back to the ponies for a pause.

Here was a truly peculiar invention: a 1,000-kilometer race on twenty-five wild ponies, a new steed for every 40-kilometer stage to ensure the endurance fell on the humans, not the horses. A Pony Express–style format that mimicked Chinggis Khan's postal system but seemed from afar more like a perfect hodgepodge of Snakes and Ladders and the Tour de France on unknown bicycles. A competition they deemed "the world's longest and toughest horse race."

I moved the mouse back into the page and worked out there were seven weeks until the start gun. The entry portal seemed to still be open, despite the deadline having passed.

Mustn't squish the mole that lives in my heart.

"Apply"—click.

II

Why do humans put so much thought into some decisions yet plunge into others like penguins into freezing ocean? Are we met with a sudden urge to avoid the direct path to middle age and subsequent visions of growing old in a lonely world of cats? I certainly have a fear of falling into the routines of my elders—their eggshell worlds of dangers and do-nots. But maybe I had a simpler desire to settle something unsaid, away from home. Or a longing to be wild and snort about like a horse.

No single reason seems satisfactory. I want to hand myself over to something, but I can't tell what creates that need to leap nor what decides its timing.

In fact, maybe this was me at age eighteen: a bundle of urges, a series of plunges. I was loud and quick. I thrived on being the loser in the anecdotes I recounted—caught without a ticket on the Underground, shouted at unjustly by an anxious teacher. I bent the world this way and that—schlepping barefoot through London,

ROUGH MAGIC · 7

to school in my pajamas, where I threw pens in class and blurted my frankest thoughts. What, besides a diagnosis of attention seeking, did any of this point to? I couldn't yet tell.

If the fashion in which I applied to and signed on for the Mongol Derby was characteristically thoughtless, the event itself would, perversely, leave me deep in thought. Grasses and a blue-domed sky. Bodies and wind and rain and pain. Wide, open prairies, and twenty-five ponies saying, *Who are you?* and *Who are we?*

By the time I took the return planes to London, words were tumbling out of me. In the writing I could mull the matter over, as a cow ruminates her grass. We had been given ten days to ride twenty-five semiwild ponies a long way around Mongolia. Why the need to go all that way and do such a thing?

I am telling a story about myself. There's a British disease called modesty, which nearly stops me from sharing what I've written. After all, this is about an event that seemed to go well. Somehow, implausibly, against the odds, I won a race labeled the longest and toughest in the world—a race I'd entered on a whim—and became the youngest person and first female ever to have done so. We read of sporting victories in the newspapers, but what about all we cannot see? It's easy to forget the thudded moments of hopelessness involved in a journey, one's deepest difficulties slowly made clear.

III

"She is *not* going to Mongolia, Julia! Julia, do you hear me?"

My father had discovered my plan to ride in the world's longest horse race and was insistent I wouldn't go. I listened from the next room as he bellowed at Mum in the kitchen.

"It's too"—his foot stomped the floor—"opportunistic!"

Dad had encouraged opportunism in the past, but when it came to horses, he was keen for me to steer clear. He often told people how he'd made it a condition of marriage that my mother give up horse riding. Years after the summer of the Derby, I would overhear him shouting at her once more. "Lara's been to Stanford University, Julia. I am *not* having her riding horses."

My father, Simon, is a large-foreheaded man with Victorian characteristics, who grew up alongside his horse-mad sister, Lucinda. He is anti-riding, anti-horses: *waste of time, waste of money* (*and* please *don't talk about them at mealtimes*). Aunt Lucinda's Olympic riding career had coincided with their father going into overdraft, while Dad worked long hours in the City. The story of him tying his sister to the oak tree when they were little circulates frequently in the family.

"Julia, are you listening?" I heard him move closer to Mum at the sink.

Lodged in the thicket of my father's anger, we would often find ourselves flapping with no clear way out. Mum quietly carried on with the washing up. If my father is a man who speaks clearly and interrupts often, my mother can be the catatonic opposite.

"Oh, I like prattling in the background," she says whenever I tell her she's mumbling, though she once followed up by saying, "I think I need to go on an assertiveness course."

Mum is generally taken with the idea of horses (my older brothers used to jest that she married Dad just to get closer to his sister) and had been all wide-eyed when I first mentioned the Mongol Derby to her. Although my father's fury had me bracing myself, it also summoned a sense of victory, since his anger seemed to speak from a powerlessness. Simon had no way of preventing me from going to Mongolia.

It seemed you needed to know how to ride to do this race, but the type of riding you did—the particular discipline—didn't matter. I couldn't say I myself had grown up riding—my parents did not ride, nor did my three brothers. Although Aunt Lucinda set me up with lessons when I pleaded for them aged seven, I lived and went to school in the city so horses were confined to Saturdays. More recently I'd been able to try Lucinda's sport, eventing, but that only required riding for a mere hour or two at a time. A month after my nineteenth birthday, I would arrive in Ulaanbaatar, the capital of Mongolia, to discover that half the Derby competitors were experienced in endurance, which involved riding up to 160 kilometers from dawn until dusk. I had never even heard of such a sport.

One of my father's fears had always been that I might turn out to be a horsewoman like his sister. Unfortunately for him, by my teenage years I sneezed and itched when around the creatures—symptoms of uncontainable excitement rather than an allergy—and could possibly be classified as a pony girl: I dreamed of saucy centaurs. I'd once hallucinated, while sober, an azure blue horse cantering towards me. And I was truly taken with the romance of those rolling English parklands where my aunt laid down her horse histories.

Yet my equestrian imagination was tethered to my urban home, a hearty part of me city-slick, London-sly. My schoolfriends and I grew up fast in the capital, leaping across it alone on the Tube and pacing its streets with elastic courage. But I felt empty in the concrete nowheres. Truly, I only loved the city for letting me leave—on Fridays, we eased our way out through darkened traffic jams, arriving centuries later in the village of Appleshaw.

Appleshaw floats in a shallow valley where the tameness of Hampshire stops and the wilds of Wiltshire begin. Weekends there sent me out to make mud-balls with my brothers, walk miles without purpose, and swim away from time. The city basin, tasked with curating our futures, drew us back every Sunday night. My brothers and I slotted into the week as dirty plates do into a dishwasher. The routine days crawled by until the eventual swing back to Appleshaw on Friday, holy Friday.

In this way, privilege had us always on the move, and it shaped me—an in-betweener ungrounded, too spacey for London, too colorful for the country, probably suspended in particles above some motorway between the two. Certainly the M3 has more of me than most places do.

Within a week of my application, Katy, the Mongol Derby organizer, returned from plotting the course on the steppe and sent me an acceptance email. I might've been gleeful were it not for the phenomenal entry fee. She said most riders had entered the previous year with sponsorship secured. For several nights, preparing to let the dream decay with the remaining magnolia leaves.

There's no knowing why Katy gave me 50 percent off when I asked for a discount, nor why she granted another $650 off when I couldn't afford the halved amount. Maybe it had something to do with the fact that I had name-dropped my aunt, Lucinda Green, on my application—Katy turned out to be a "bit of a fan." Or perhaps it was my opening sentence: *I am extremely competitive and want to become the youngest (am 18) person to finish.*

I trotted down to the bank with my head held delusionally high and poured out a lifelong collection of pennies from my checkered plastic pig, hoping they would top up my balance to near enough the asked-for price. Prior to that, I had refused to spend any of my savings, and it's endearing to me now that I was willing to hand all of it over for a horse race I might not last very long in.

I was expecting quite the holiday—a green steppe stuffed full of feisty ponies, with hunky riders from all over the world. One to trump the sightseeing and sunbathing holidays I was used to. Earlier that year I had wound my way through India, stopping at temples highlighted by a Lonely Planet guidebook, viewing the world through a manicured prism as any good tourist does—but my eyes had run out of space. By the time I applied for the Derby, I was no longer keen on touring the world's buildings with awestruck stares. My thighs were strong and my heart was raw, yearning for my own motion.

IV

"You won't enjoy it."

I held my tongue.

"Sure," the voice on the telephone continued, "it's phenomenal, but the accidents last year were horrific. Google them."

It was high July when I rang Lucy, a past competitor. Down the line came factual splatter: *broken ribs, amputated finger, cracked pelvises, punctured lung, torn ligaments, broken collarbones.* On she went as I watched a ladybird crawl up the lamp at my side: *bucking ponies, fraying girths, sicknesses, extreme dehydration, getting lost, not fun, don't expect fun.*

I couldn't just slump there in that dusty Appleshaw chair and roll my eyes. Mongolia was coming for me in a month.

How many riders finished the race during her year?

"I think thirty-five of us started. . . . Seventeen finished."

I thanked her and said goodbye, feeling my wrist wilt as I

dropped the phone back onto the receiver. I wanted to pull out of the race. Summer had swallowed its charm.

In the kitchen I told my older brother Arthur the news as he traipsed on by.

"Oh my." He shivered and dashed upstairs, relieved not to be me.

I could not pull out of the race—I had paid for it and written letters asking for charitable donations in the name of it—so I let the terror energize me instead. Asked afterwards if I would dare attempt the race again, I'd reply that I could never again be scared enough to do so. The supernatural power of fearing the unknown stunned me into a state of readiness. With four weeks to go, I launched my attack.

Although my application claimed I'd been riding five horses a day, this was fiction. I had been au pairing the toddler in Austria.

"Never too late," declared Mum as she poured herself another cup of tea.

I volunteered at the local stud, where I began riding three or four horses a day. I also started playing tennis again and running farther than usual. It is a horse's habit to pace about when she feels a storm approaching. Winding herself up seems to ready her for the coming saga. Now that I've forgotten the accompanying terror, I long for the manic flurry of those July days, hopping from horse to horse as I edged towards the race. The whole affair indulged my existence.

Bartramia, a small and racy gray, was the closest creature to a Mongolian pony I could find at the stud. I rode her through all the valleys—even rode her bareback once. Her canter quickened as my calves clung to her full-moon tummy, my boots ripping through the knee-high ragwort. Onwards she flew, a wood ahead, no sign of slowing.

"Woah!" I shouted into the wind at her ears—could I bear this for 1,000 kilometers? "Woah now!"

At the last second she jinked left, braking on the turn as my chest jolted over her shoulders, leaving me hanging on with my thighs as she picked up her gallop again, on up the hill along the rim of the woods.

This was the terrible thrill. Come August I would encounter it atop twenty-five wilder ponies, free of the tightly bound English fields. Our Mongolian ponies would be the descendants of Genghis Khan's famed Takhi horses, who shouldered his empire's postal system from the thirteenth century onwards. Their speed allowed letters from Siberia to arrive in Poland within twelve days, though our ride wouldn't go beyond the border of Mongolia's green oasis—a wide island surrounded by the Gobi Desert to the south, the barren Altai Mountains to the west, and the freezing wastelands of Siberia on the northern border with Russia.

I had begun to notice how the idea of Mongolia made many a Brit go quiet. I don't think the reason is Genghis Khan as much as the void in our history. Where British culture has not forced its influence, we tread carefully, sensing a different lay of the land. England was crafted by roads and fields, flooded with a web of happenings with which I was familiar. The steppe would strip all this away.

V

The race was set to begin on August 4. In the first week of July, the organizers sent me a month-by-month "Your Year of the Derby" calendar. They had sent this to everyone else at the beginning of the year, since they had applied on time. We were advised to assemble our gear in February, get vaccinated in April, commence language-learning in May, use July to visit relatives and update our wills, and devote the entire year to training.

Maggie, an endurance-riding specialist, had apparently been sending handouts on fitness, navigation, horse pacing, and hydration. "You've missed those now and it's too late for you to be training anyway. You can't get fitter in the final two weeks," she stated on the telephone. I gulped and clung closer to the daft resistance within me.

The month-by-month calendar from the organizers read: *You could do all your preparation in July if you have unusually low blood pressure—no? Thought not.*

I do happen to have low blood pressure, and a low heart rate. Perhaps that would help. When I was small and we measured our vital signs in class, Mrs. Bleakley said my results meant either I was an athlete, or I was nearly dead, or I couldn't count. Likely the latter—despite being a decade older when I entered the race, I still struggled with numbers and time.

July rolled by. I researched all the race's sore statistics and found that Lucy was right. Every year just over half the field made it to the finish. No woman had ever won the Derby, nor had a Briton. South Africans tended to triumph. The youngest person ever to cross the finish line had been twenty-three.

Me? I was not young. I had long since given up my rubber ducklings, I had finished high school, I felt ancient as a walnut.

Meanwhile, my father had forgotten his resistance. He helped me draft letters to family and friends asking for contributions to the charities I had chosen to ride in the name of—Macmillan Cancer Support and Greenhouse Sports. The latter, which sets up sports programs for London teenagers struggling with school, was a charity that amazed me, perhaps because sport had felt like my own lifeline in the city.

I needed to focus on this campaign before departure. No one would donate when I returned from the race having managed only 10 of the 1,000 expected kilometers. Aware now that the other riders had signed up for the Derby in October, giving them ten months to train and plan how much toilet paper to pack, I implied in my letters that I, too, had been aiming at the race for about a year.

✦

When I was young, Dad had often called me "Sporty Mouse." I was flat-chested and athletic enough that you couldn't tell me apart from my brothers. In fact, as far as I was concerned, I was a boy. I existed in the mold of my siblings. I scorned at girly-girls with Barbies and bolted from pink, that color of social catastrophe— sickly and sweet, nothing like me. I sat best with blue, the color of distance and coldness, the favorite of my brothers and mother, too. "Where's my willy?" I demanded of her in the bath at age three. She and I have hair growing out of us in surprising places. She says the forests on my legs and the two-inch hair growing by my belly button mean I'm strong.

The other half of the picture is one I tended to ignore. Mum sometimes referred to me as "Sensitive Mouse." My stomach has ached since I was fifteen, I blush all the time, and my skin rashes red when you so much as brush a finger over it. You know what they say about thin-skinned people: a highly strung, sensitive lot, prone to withering like flowers in winter. Doctors do not prescribe them 1,000-kilometer horse races.

We were supposed to have seen the warning on the website before signing up:

> Before you consider applying for this race, we want to point out how dangerous the Mongol Derby is. By taking part in this race you are greatly increasing your risk of severe physical injury or even death. The nature of the Derby means that if you do fall off, the response time of the medics is going to depend on where you are. If you are seriously injured you may be hundreds of miles away from

the nearest hospital. The Mongol Derby is an extremely physically demanding and dangerous race, and holds the title as the toughest horse race in the world for good reason.

I had missed it.

I didn't understand the coming race, and wouldn't until I rode in it. I did, however, assume that something would go wrong for all of us riding and that we would need to step back and ponder the silliness. After all, didn't entering such a competition demand a deviant imagination? Could we envisage ordinary days blown from their moorings? Could we pretend that moving through space with unbearable intensity had been a natural habit our whole lives?

Even some of the Mongolian parents I would meet, whose eight-year-old children could gallop for hours without saddles, thought the 1,000-kilometer distance crazy. No wonder, then, that the race had been thought up elsewhere—by a man in Bristol called Tom Morgan. Tom found out that the steppe's medieval messaging systems were still in place until the 1960s, and with the guidance of an original postal rider, he helped stage the first Mongol Derby five years before I entered. The race had since grown, and was now summoning a field of thirty to forty riders annually.

VI

I like to laugh matters into detachment, but I found the approaching monster tricky to belittle. A week before my departure for Mongolia, I lay in bed thinking about William the Conqueror. How mad of him to risk visiting England with an army in 1066.

Me, 947 years later: No desire to conquer. Merely wanting to leave Normandy, as it were. Live a little.

Half an hour after these musings, across a breakfast table laden with tropical fruit, my godfather, Michel, lowered his newspaper to make an announcement.

"No one wins the Tour before their early thirties. . . ."

The man knows about endurance sport, having competed in Olympic luge and, more recently, cycled Tour de France sportives.

"They haven't developed the combination of mental and physical toughness," he continued, turning his bold gaze to me. "You—what are you—nineteen?"

This kind of pinpointing tended to prompt my rebellion and

excitement. But next to me I noticed my mother's mouth slowing down as she chewed, her forehead rising into wrinkles. The person who often did not notice when she lost her six-year-old daughter in the supermarket as she floated along, silently focusing on the goat's cheese—the person who bicycles blindly across main roads, leaving traffic to swerve out of her way—began now to engage with the reality of the race.

A few days later, I walked over to Aunt Lucinda's to borrow some equipment. I must've expected some advice, too—she was my go-to ahead of any equestrian event. She lived 150 meters away from us in Appleshaw.

Aunt Lucinda never likes to concentrate fully on one thing, so she was weeding the gravel in her driveway when she hollered some last words to me.

"I suspect you won't make it past day three but don't be disappointed."

She raced inside to get me a can of Anti Monkey Butt—some powder for sore bottoms she had discovered in America—and waved me away, yelling she had to fly. She was on her way to Austria for teaching.

This kind of perennial rush might be a family trend. We flee from the waiting, lest it confronts us with some startling boredom. If we really questioned why, though, I'm not sure we'd have an answer. Maybe rushing is a symptom of self-importance, or a fear of getting close to others, lest they shatter us.

Although Aunt Lucinda lived across the road, her house, which arrived flat-packed on a lorry from Scandinavia in the 1980s, was almost always deserted. I was frustrated by the absences of my champion aunt, whose achievements held a mythic place in my rural imagination. She earns her living flying around the world teaching people how to ride cross-country, saying things like "Squeeze the horse like a tube of toothpaste. Not too hard, we don't want it all coming out at once."

What I couldn't accept was that it might be difficult for a champion to lay her head on the same pillow each night, since the glorious memories might only be going stale. It must, I suppose, be easier to be consumed by airplanes, hopping between sites of forgetful newness.

Even on the ground, Lucinda advances in quick, short strides, as if awakened by a storm. Apparently her mum once told her, "Being mother to you is like being mother to a lightning conductor."

After I left her that day, she sent me a text reading *Xxxxxxx*. This is the type of message she sends when at a loss as to what to advise.

From an old history teacher, I had a short email: *I've heard from people that know people that they eat testicles in Mongolia.* And that was it.

It didn't surprise me that no one was taking my race attempt seriously. I was that scatterbrain who lost Oyster cards on the Underground and failed driving tests. "I find it difficult to park between the lines," I explained to my eldest brother, George, who has been serious about cars, and many other things, since the age of four.

"You don't even know where the lines are," he said.

What was it that kept them all from trusting me—not with the keys, the cars, the dogs? Nor with time? The not trusting meant *bits missing. Lara's got bits missing. She's not fully here.* She's a clock without some numbers, a clock who forgets to tick. I trusted myself a little at least, suspecting the missing bits were waiting for me somewhere. Certainly I had felt flashes when I went to get those chickens from Dorset on the train. Ticktocks sounding out in my core.

It is too late to get fit, too late to pull out, but not too late to organize kit. With five days to go, the lights are out in the kitchen as I draw a stick figure of my Derby self and label the clothes I'll wear on each plot of body, ticking off my bottom first. The super-padded knickers have arrived and seem good—larger than granny pants, fatter than boxing gloves. Every day I mold my stubborn bunions— big bone onions, my witchiest features—into my new secondhand trekking boots. For other stuff, I am deep into bargaining wars on eBay, tending towards items cheaply made in China. Many will decompose during the race, maps and water bottles flying out of my broken pockets across the windy plains. I begin scribbling a list of things to pack.

1. Me
2. I like lists
3. I can be orderly
4. I do love lists
5. And so I stumble
6. Like a poem unfurling

When the day came to peel myself from the British Isles, summer was high, the best plums were ripening, and all the grass looked Wimbledon-worthy. These commonplace things I had rarely noticed before transformed themselves into snippets of certainty, their impending disappearances conjuring my new appreciation.

I'd discovered, via Facebook, that a certain competitor had

been thrown a send-off dinner at which she was presented with a horse-shaped cake wishing her good luck. Seeing how the race could merit celebration before its first kilometer had been ridden leant me a sense of achievement, although my own departure was not a public affair.

My father blasted my mother and me out of the house, fretful, as usual, that we might be late for the airport. In the terminal Mum shed tears, which were, as always, saddening to receive. I sometimes think of her as a balloon not entirely tied to earth—she drifts along until the concluding point, when her emotions burst out. I myself did not weep. I was leaping out to Mongolia to ride in a giant horse race. It was either too much, or nothing at all.

VII

Beneath the plane window the steppe folded in green waves. As we descended, white tents appeared at valley mouths, met by colorful tin-roofed houses flowing down the gullies towards gray high-rises. The plane let me out in Ulaanbaatar, 8,000 kilometers away from home.

Through the taxi glass I saw fragments of a city. Men in big coats curled around fires, denim-clad figures spilled into the traffic. Small-windowed blocks stood alongside nomads' tents at the outskirts; farther in, Soviet architecture leaned into slicker glass structures. By now there was no sign of the steppe. The only hint of horses rested on the tögrög—the Mongolian currency—that I handed to the taxi driver: wild-maned ponies cantered off the banknote edges.

At four the next morning I sat sleepless in a hotel room among bloated white pillows. Delving into my suitcase, I pulled out a collection of tangled ropes and confused penknives that had spent their lives dormant in my brothers' drawers. There was also a copy of *The Tempest*, which I had taken no interest in at school, but after leaving found myself diving into for comfort. Shakespeare speaks another language, yet I never needed to know the whole meaning to be moved by the sounds—Caliban's "I cried to dream again" moves me to real tears.

My eleven-year-old self, on the other hand, did not spare the play a thought—I was pursuing real commotion. There was nothing like the sound of Mr. Thompson's angry voice soaring. "Get out," he'd shout, when he caught me whisper-giggling. "I said, 'Get. Out.'" In the wasteland of the corridor I would lean against the wall while the pink in my cheeks faded, unaware that in the play I'd left on my desk were a series of rebellions I might have admired.

Now I lay on the floor of that sublimely square hotel room ripping out soliloquies and gluing them into my flimsy Winnie-the-Pooh notebook. I imagined they'd live out the race in my backpack and might lift me out of any lows. *U just have to get through the pain with . . . poetry*, Mum had written in an email that midnight, British time.

VIII

The following morning, competitors met for the first time. Stuffed into a corporate room in the city, ours was a silence of not quite wanting to begin. Horses seem to do these things better. On meeting, they amble and sniff bottoms. Sometimes they squeal.

In the 1930s, John Steinbeck embarked on a scientific research trip to the Sea of Cortez. Reflecting on his fellow crew members, he wrote, "None of us was possessed of the curious boredom within ourselves which makes adventurers or bridge players." Were we a handful of those people who cannot sit still? Or were we all seeking the great death? I believe we sought some kind of oblivion. The characters in *The Tempest* leap from their sinking ship in a "fever of the mad."

Maybe we desired a heroic proving. I was aware there were people in the world who classified themselves as adventurers, inhabiting the realm of the extreme, dog-panting for epics and gagging for photos in Gore-Tex. I didn't know how many were here, or whether I was about to become one. The "longest, toughest" superlative had surely appealed to many, though I've conveniently erased from memory whether or not it had been a draw for me personally. What would my eleven-year-old self think of me buying into such a constructed adventure?

As the hello-how-are-yous of the crew piled onto one another, I spotted Maggie, the race steward, at the head of the room. She had mattresses of curly red hair. In a phone conversation two weeks prior, she'd told me that I "frankly" didn't sound prepared. She was not to take me seriously until the finish line, and even then her eyes would search me with the same unconvinced look, a sort of shock that I'd ever made it beyond the borders of my mother's vegetable patch.

The day was made up of a series of briefings on the race. The veterinarians explained horses' hydration levels, gut sounds, lameness protocol, and heart rates. Pushing horses too hard would lead to elevated rates. The rules imposed a two-hour penalty or race expulsion if a horse's heart rate remained above 64 beats per minute for a period longer than forty-five minutes after the end of each leg.

"Look—after—your—horse," concluded the Scottish vet.

It seemed simple enough, though it hadn't crossed my mind you could take a horse's heart rate, let alone how four hours' exercise might change that rate.

During a break, the paramedic handed out medical forms. I didn't meet his gaze as I handed the paper back to him, uneasy about its incompleteness. Aunt Lucinda is a stickler for eye contact. If I manage to look her in the eye when she's telling me off, she congratulates me later (such is her stick-and-carrot formula), but I find focusing difficult.

"I haven't had a rabies vaccine. I'm sorry. I'm not sure what these other ones are."

His mouth opened. Apparently the steppe was teeming with rabid dogs. I'd not had time for the recommended vaccinations before departure.

"Not even hepatitis A?"

Was that a sexually transmitted disease? I slunk away.

Bureaucracy flapped on like a beached fish—riders weighed, papers signed, headshots taken. By the lunchtime talk, "Rules of the Race," the room understood itself a little better. The Derby (they went on) was an unsupported one-stage race, but riding would be limited to the hours between 7 a.m. and 8:30 p.m., outside of which we'd be penalized. Positions were policed by rider satellite trackers, which would also allow people to follow the race on the internet. There was no set route, only twenty-five obligatory horse-changing stations, where we would choose our next steeds. Those stations changed every year, and the course had been kept secret until today, when we were handed map books with wiggly red lines on each page.

By the time Maggie and Katy, the organizer who discounted my entry fee, leaned back in their armchairs and opened the floor for questions, I had grown comfortable enough in my seat to share some qualms. I raised an arm and waited.

"Will anyone be waking us up in the mornings?"

My voice was meek, as if I'd emerged from a breathless swim in a chlorine pool. These voices—the chlorine edition is just one—bring themselves up from my internal cellar and pour forth, unfiltered.

The room cackled more with amazement than amusement. They didn't know my alarm clock was an untrustable brand of wristwatch from a French supermarket. The panel, including

Maggie, barely answered. "One fool can ask more questions than ten wise men can answer"—so says a Mongolian proverb.

My tongue asked the next question without me. "If you're with a partner and one of you falls, can you both ride one horse?"

Heads swung around. I vacated my face as though my words weren't intentional. I wanted to feel out the limits of this strange race. The panel admitted to having no rule against my proposition. As usual, I could sense everyone else in the room but had no grasp of myself—not of how I appeared, nor of what I might do next. Pixie mode is automatic, a relic from school, released to tickle any uptight armpits in a room. She was born, this pixie inside me, in response to an atmosphere of seriousness.

On she went, wondering aloud, "So you could do the whole thing in a truck? With each of the twenty-five ponies successively loaded into the boot?"

Frowns met frowns, a few stragglers laughing. In this way, the beginning quickly slipped from my control. That the great race was a bit ridiculous—that we were in danger of forgetting this—seemed to be the idea hiding behind my questions, but those questions probably just prompted other riders to decide I was delusional. Never mind. The following day would cast us into the grasslands.

I walked back to the hotel. Wet streets sobbed the summer away, waiting for the winter to return with a duvet of snow. A thin lady strutted past me, coatless, perhaps unused to her own bare arms. Ulaanbaatar sits at a coordinate where the cold lasts for much of the year, long enough that the marmots outside the city begin growing new coats immediately after shedding them in July.

The city hadn't found a place in my foreign vision of Mongolia, yet half the country's population lives in Ulaanbaatar. Many people have recently moved in from the steppe to trade products they once produced such as meat and wool. The city itself moved twenty-eight times before settling at its current location in 1778. What was once a mobile monastery is now a metropolis of solid foundation, no more, or less, nomadic than London or Beijing.

No one hung about for long on the lively main street. I felt hidden among people, of whom there would soon be few, and beneath buildings, of which there would soon be none.

IX

Evening brought hard rain and wide-mouthed puddles. The competitors reconvened at an Indian restaurant in the city's southeast, where I sat on a stool next to a gray-haired man named Paddy, an amateur race jockey with a family of four. His Irish accent was a lullaby to my rigid English ears. On my other side was a wooden pillar supporting the sloped ceiling, whose lack of conversation I became grateful for as dinner droned on. The thirty competitors spewed out Derby secrets as they slurped Indian cuisine. I learned a great deal about Indian food and about riding 1,000 kilometers.

"That's *dal*, a lentil dish. . . ."

"So, always take the tracks around the mountains—it's the best route. . . . *Phwooof*, you won't handle the spice in this curry."

Paddy and Chloe, a rider from New Zealand, answered all my questions generously. Maybe they had visions of my clumsy frame falling from a pony the very next day.

As food circulated, I tuned into an American voice—that of a blond girl I'd noticed in the briefing room, where she had sat at the front, arching her body back to laugh during the army doctor's presentation. She'd drawn widespread attention at the afternoon's end when an Australian competitor fainted and she remarked, "Well, we're not all going to make it to the start line."

Here she was at dinner talking about her Derby coach. A coach? Specifically designed for one of the world's least-known sporting events? Brought to the dinner table in oral form? I shot looks at bright-eyed Kiwi Chloe.

By now I knew the American's name—Devan Horn—and was fast separating it from my associations with Devon, the gently rolling English county.

"If I don't finish the race in six days, I'm not going home," continued Devan, adding that she would "imprison" herself on the steppe if she didn't meet her goal. Should we hang our heads low, or decree her abominable? It sounded hard enough to finish within the ten-day limit.

No one was sure whether this Devan actually had a chance of winning or if her talents were limited to the oratory game. I diverted my attention to Chloe's unassuming discussion of jodhpurs.

"Mine are Lycra."

"Mine are full chaps," chipped in Paddy.

What to say? "Mine have padding on the inside seams."

Devan leaned across the table, replanting herself in the conversation. "Wow, padding? Watch out. You're gonna get a huge welt pretty quick . . ."

I looked across at her, miffed.

". . . like *this* size," she finished.

Perhaps she was looking out for me. But her lips were pursed as she gestured a shape the size of a mango, emphasizing the enormity of my incoming welt. I retired from dinner and bedded down by my books to dream of rotting legs.

Devan's tactic was admirable and, dare I say, age-old. On the campaign trail, Genghis Khan's soldiers lit campfires, mounted dummies on spare horses, and trailed branches and bushes—all to create the impression their numbers were far greater than they actually were. I don't know if Devan's intimidation was intentional. It certainly lent me some fear. And if fear had propelled me through the July preparations, it might now be my undoing.

X

On the bus out to the steppe, where we would spend two days pre-race training, I felt I had landed myself a comrade. Natacha ("My name is spelled with a C not an S, actually") had grown up in Paris and, like me, had a handful of brothers. At nineteen, we were among the youngest competitors attempting the race. Our hasty friendship rested on these shared facts. She chattered with a darting, expectant expression as the city fell away out the window.

I had tried not to let anyone know my age. I was young, and young is foreign. *Never* trust a teenager. It was novel for me to be socializing with adults on equal terms, especially under the pretense that I could compete with them. The sport of horseback riding values experience more than youthful daring; athletes reach their peak later than they might do in other sports. Over the years, the average age of Mongol Derby competitors had been thirty-five. I feared no one would want to ride alongside a nineteen-year-old, although I'd heard that by the age of fourteen, Genghis Khan had killed one of his half brothers in a fight over hunting spoils—a horrid story, but a promising one too.

As Natacha talked on, I fell asleep. When I woke from my snooze, the bus had left the road to rumble across grassland. About 150 kilometers southwest of Ulaanbaatar, we drew into our training camp, a series of tents and a marquee lying beneath a crescent-shaped ridge. The ridge overlooked a vast plain draped in mist, beyond which mountains kept their distance. At night, as we lay in our little tents, the mist would increase, as if asking me to notice my dread.

That afternoon, though, we spilled from the bus and rushed to the tents like ducks to bread. I left my belongings on a patch of grass and glanced about. At the corners of my vision two horses were grazing. Green stretched in all directions, met at the horizon by blue sky. This seemed more of a space than a place, shapeless and free. I kept looking around expecting the ocean to roll in.

If there is one piece of furniture crucial to imagining the Mongolian steppe, it's the *ger*, meaning "home" in Mongolian. Usually pronounced "gaire" without the long vowel (almost *grr*), it is the Mongolian equivalent of the Russian yurt: a white, circular felt tent that looks like a giant muffin crossed with a hot-air balloon. A ger is no bigger than your thumb in front of your face. Each one has a tin chimney sticking out of the center. There are no windows, for these are homes to turn you in on yourself, to let you forget the unkempt spaciousness outside them. Gers are cool in summer and warm in winter, when cow dung heats the central stove. A thin chimney takes smoke from the stove out of the top of the ger. For some shamans, this chimney is symbolic of the "world tree," a link between the alternate realities of the underworld and the upper world.

Genghis (or, more correctly, Chinggis) Khan is also known as the "unifier of the people of the felt-walled tents" in Mongolian. Gers rarely change in size: this is not cottage versus castle. Before the communist takeover, the last ruler of Mongolia sipped tea in a ger as humble as everyone else's.

A few times a year, nomadic families in Mongolia pack up their gers and move through the land in search of better pasture. Contrary to popular perception, nomads have fixed circuits—they are not drifters, and will return to similar places each year.

I imagine gers require less effort to move than brick houses, since they're collapsible within the hour, and the families I would meet on my journey rarely had more than three. After their passing, apparently you would hardly know they'd been. The respect for nature, or *baigal*—"what exists"—is such that many Mongolians on the steppe wear shoes with soft, curved soles to spare the stalks of the tiniest plants and to avoid hurting the earth.

XI

It is the first day of training. I stick a tentative foot through the stirrup and focus on the herder's bushy mustache. As I prepare to pull myself up, gripping the pony's wrinkled mane, I remind myself it *is* just a horse—a solid, four-legged, hairy, plant-eating, sometimes-domesticated mammal with a mane and tail. Yet my breath is scared.

I think I felt more fear in that cold-blooded moment than I would at any point in the race. I didn't show it. I was attached to my exterior of fearlessness. Even inside my head, I never went near phrases such as "I am scared," "I am sad," or "I am angry." Perhaps this failure to emotionally engage linked me to the long tradition of British adventurers who refused to let anything flummox them, even if their partner's leg fell off in the Arctic. I imagine this sort of disconnection from emotion was also required by their contemporaries and forebears when running an often brutal empire. Somehow, I cannot separate myself from that history.

The pony was tiny, yet standing at his side I felt the cumulative danger of all the risky times I'd ever experienced with horses. I had been led to believe Mongolian ponies were especially life-threatening. Despite standing half asleep on the horse lines, they were rarely handled and therefore hypersensitive to human motion. If you were lucky to get on board, you would, I'd been told, certainly have no control thenceforth.

The Right to Buck Off a Human Being is one of what I think of as the universal horse rights. Competitors had broken bones from such treatment at past training camps. Years earlier, I myself had broken my collarbone off a horse named Tweenie, whose sensational buck had her known locally as The Witch, a label I loved her for.

The pony did not move when I mounted. It turned out the start-camp horses had been tamed to prevent a repeat of the previous year's injuries. "Choo choo," said the herder, using the equivalent of a cowboy's "giddy-up." My pony fell into a donkey trot.

Riding is a dance that demands each muscle in your body answer to an ever-shifting floor. If you speak the language of trot, you will know it as the least graceful of pony paces. I rose up and down to the jarring rhythm, my vision underlined by a pair of triangular ears. If there is a grandeur associated with horseback riding, there was none here. Crawling around the basin aboard our short-legged ponies, we thrust our chests outwards, and with every rising stride, the giant, noncommittal landscape erased us.

✦

As the sun dropped behind the ridge, I stooped through the door of the ger at the end of the row. Soft-spoken Paddy and four others were already roosting on low beds, indulging in yet another Lycra discussion. Matthias, a forty-year-old who lay with his headlamp glowing, muttered in his German accent, "I don't wear Dri-FIT clothes. After three days, I start to feel like a sausage."

I fell asleep to the noises of a party in full tilt. Someone stumbled in after midnight and collapsed next to me, snoring menacingly. From the outline of a beard I decided it had to be Todd, who herded cattle in Australia for a living and smoked a lot of cigarettes.

The next morning, Natacha chirpily repeated the pleas of an Australian voice she had overheard behind her tent in the night: "Look, listen. I love your bum, I love your boobs, and I fucking love your personality. . . . Now just hurry up and sleep with me."

He was talking, Natacha suspected, to one of the vets, who did not sound keen on his advances.

At dawn on the second training day, I got entangled in my backpack, which required the rescue of three crew members, including a thickset, heavily eyebrowed man in his early thirties called Charles. The test pony then sprang me over the plain with weathered resolve, but the saddlebag soon fell off, causing him to have a bucking fit. I jumped off before he threw me.

Beneath the pony's tummy, I sat untying the bag from his upper back leg, as though this were my beach spot, and he my parasol. My tent-mates abandoned me in their hurry to reach the training checkpoint, and Richard, the official race photographer, drove across the plain to magnify his view of my situation. He muttered from his jeep window as he pulled up, an easy smile behind his words.

I mumbled back. "No, I do not know where to go. I can't read my GPS. Is it the pink line or the blue line or the red dot? What's that arrow? Me? Really?"

I had been expecting, and am still expecting, someone to teach me how to use a global positioning system. Although there are many maps of Mongolia, there were no suitable GPS maps at the time of the race. I liked the idea of traversing a space free of the net of lines I associated with maps. The organizers had entered the coordinates of the horse-changing stations into our GPS system, but no one had mentioned what the numbers and colors meant.

I often feel strange in groups, overwhelmed by the puzzle of humans, so I was moping at the back when the next lot of riders decided to take a deliciously straight line over the rocky ridge. Like a good sheep I went after them, ignoring the alternative track skirting the mountain. At the top, my horse refused to descend. Like the last lot, the others went on without me.

Marooned on the peak, I dismounted and slung my body down on the stone crumble. I wasn't aware of any rules for the training day so, relieved from the group-hurry, I began dozing. In this state I occasionally returned to the problem at hand, erupting in a spate of giggles. I hadn't noticed until now that part of me preferred to travel slowly and catastrophically. Nor had I realized this preference would be at odds with participating in a race. Later I would learn that Devan, the well-prepared American competitor, was by now already back at camp, bulging her eyes out of her skull at the news of our group so stupidly going over the ridge.

When I was sixteen my favorite history teacher told me to start taking myself seriously. I loved her, so I tried to listen, but I didn't understand people who took things seriously. I especially loathed the Head Girl team, who flapped their wings like mother hens and mowed the school corridors with gravity. I couldn't see why you would invest in life in this fashion. How did serious people fare when the world turned around to surprise them?

Hours later, I returned to find Devan holding court on the grass. When she announced she was taking bids from people to ride with her, Tom, a tall, blond twenty-four-year-old American, casually said he might like to join Team Devan.

She looked him up and down from her sacred patch of land. "Sure. If you can keep up."

By the next morning, Tom would have torn ligaments in his shoulder, not at the hands of Devan, but because he'd had the pluck to take on a Mongolian in a nighttime wrestling match. The fact that wrestling was the national sport in Mongolia had not been noted by Tom, a risk analyst by trade. What foresight Devan seemed to have.

My own race plans were vested in a six-meter bungee rope I had nabbed on eBay. During nights spent in the open, I would tie it from my tummy to the pony's bridle to stop the pony straying. None of the other riders believed I was serious about sleeping attached to a wild horse. They thought I'd just end up being dragged down a flinted valley and deposited in bog. It was during such conversations that I felt myself falling into their stereotypes of an English eccentric—Class B: ditzy, female. None of them were aware that I effected similar surprise back home. At the end of the first training day, a rider from California had asked if I was high, while another had simply inquired, after watching me clown about with a little boy, "Who is your mother?"

I sank back into my heart.

Once again I ate lunch beside Paddy, who narrowed his eyes and leaned into me to reveal his bet on Matthias, the German with no tolerance for Dri-FIT, as the likely winner of the race.

"That Matthias, oof, he's a real interesting guy. You know what?"

"What?"

He lowered his voice, "My money's on him to win."

Matthias and Paddy had decided to ride together. For hours that morning they flustered about the gloomy ger, packing and repacking their luggage. Matthias epitomized the winning expert, but without Devan's swagger. He did tai chi before breakfast both training mornings, had apparently lost 60 pounds before the race (riders weren't allowed to weigh more than 85 kilograms, or 187 pounds, in their gear), and had clocked up over 6,400 kilometers on lone training rides in the Australian outback with his GPS. I had never ridden more than 20 kilometers at once, let alone with a GPS, and, as established, I didn't know how to use one anyway.

On the eve of the race, we ate a sacrificed sheep, the smell of whose blood still hung about in the air when I sidled up to Devan Horn to find out a little more. She was a gap that needed filling; I'd been circling around her in conversations all day. I found her facing away from the fire with her arms crossed. She answered my queries looking straight at me, the firelight flickering up her rounded cheeks. She was studying criminology at "the third-best school for criminology in the U.S." and had grown up in Austin, Texas. She was on the U.S. national endurance riding team and "only" twenty years old. She asked me no questions. The conversation concluded with silence.

An American film crew from ABC had arrived earlier that afternoon to make a documentary of the Derby. They quickly discovered "Devan's bravado" and took wide-angled shots of her staring at the horizon in her slick purple sunglasses, the wind mopping her hair and jostling the grasses behind her.

"What's the plan, you gonna win this thing?"

She looked at the interviewer, deadpan. Universe, move out the way. Behold, Devan Horn, endurance rider from the West. "Yes."

What had we all missed by not growing up in Texas?

I think the rest of us understood we, too, needed faith in the race and in ourselves. But we were under the impression that we would need just as much doubt, since the odds were against us. Could envisaging victory, or foretelling any story, make it come true?

Well, what if the race had already happened, in all our preparatory thoughts and words, and we were simply now going to receive it?

I hummed my way back to the ger, where Paddy and Matthias were in mad-rabbit mode, flinging discarded headlamps and Mongolian phrasebooks over their shoulders. They had come lathered in death-prevention equipment but they needed now to minimize their luggage weight. Theirs was a very professional paranoia, one that rendered most alternative attitudes naive. I slid into bed and wrote in my Winnie-the-Pooh notebook, feeling I was no match for their good middle age and doubled-up mapping systems.

Matthias soon interrupted our sleep to announce he felt very smelly. I lifted my head to check if his words were real. His legs were sprawled off the end of his mattress.

"Why do you smell?" I asked.

"It's all the carbs I've been eating at this base camp," he sighed. "Making me really stinky."

Minutes later he let out a prolonged, equine groan.

XII

And as the morning steals upon the night,
Melting the darkness, so their rising senses
Begin to chase the ignorant fumes that mantle
Their clearer reason.

—*The Tempest*

What gets you out of bed? The thought of breakfast.
  What gets you out of bed? The idea there is somewhere to go.

It is the first morning of the race proper. An hour before the start
gun, the mist gives way to a weighty heat. I wander among scurrying
riders—saddles taped, ropes tied, Sesame Snaps packed—and
queue up for luggage weigh-ins with scary steward Maggie. Others
have packed a perfect 4.9 kilograms, just below the 5-kilogram

limit. My kit, dangling from the miniature scales, only weighs 3.4 kilograms. Maggie deals me a look. I sprint up to the ger and stuff in some of Paddy's unwanted toilet paper, unsure what else to take. According to one of the race organizers, Mongolians on the steppe often travel unladen, barely a vegetable in tow.

When the herder hands me the reins of a tiny gray pony, I think, Oh dear, if only I were as little. Snoozing Todd, my Australian tent-mate, waltzes over to the horse lines a few minutes after me as though it's all a giant holiday. We are the last to arrive.

My tendency for lateness comes from a fear of feeling committed when early. Even on the special occasions when I decide to be early, I still end up being late. Time is a muscle that seems to randomly flex and relax in a bid to misplace me and many others. I can't rid myself of the sensation that I'm about to fall off the back of the world, as you would fall off a treadmill.

The entity in charge of my dreams brings this theme up at least once a week. While writing about the race, I've had some specific Mongol Derby dreams in which I'm terribly behind time. In one, I can't make the decision to sign on, and when I do, I'm too late, so I just drive the race in a car through a fantastic hybrid country of futuristic San Francisco, Mongolian steppe, and rural England. In another, I'm forced to bicycle through a swimming pool to get to the start of the race in time, but I miss it anyway. Time always wins.

I swing myself on. The gray horse and I walk over to Richard, the photographer, and I ask him to lengthen the pony's bridle. I've seen other riders treating Richard with half-bowed heads—but the pony resists, butting him in the armpit as we turn away. I fear for his camera.

We move to the start line, tensed upon our horses, talking at their ears. There are stories of carnage at past race starts—ponies celebrating the gathering by flinging their backs and disposing of their riders. The pony I'm on doesn't seem the type for such theatrics. He walks in a trance, his tail swishing against space, sights of grass. *So much to eat, so little time.* Is that what they all think? He sighs.

Ahead on the plain a blue banner hangs from leaning stumps: WELCOME BRAVE RIDERS. It's a brittle sight. I am not brave, am actually very jittery—scared of the dark in the yard at home, always creeping through it in the gait of a chicken. Then again, I'm tired of the hype. Even here on the start line, I only half believe the stories about the race being so awful. A part of me is looking back up at the world from its underbelly, saying *Come along, don't be scared, there's nothing down here*, like Dad used to say from the cellar, even if it was full of deadly winter frogs.

We congregate around a red-robed lama, or "high priest," who sits cross-legged on the grass. When he begins chanting a blessing for our journey, we try to hold the ponies still, but they're fidgeting in reaction to our nerves. Todd is slurping water at my side. Bubbles slip up the plastic tube from his backpack to his mouth. He radiates the smell of last night's beer. Around us are the other twenty-nine riders. I feel the steppe inspect us: a curious bunch, a motley crowd, a sea of legs dropping from horse tummies. In one of her text messages, Aunt Lucinda worried that my long legs would drag on the ground from a Mongolian pony. She suggested I purchase roller skates to protect my feet.

Aunt and I did not part on the best of terms. The day before she went to Austria, I decided to rub some sweat off her horse's tummy while she was near his head, which upset him enough to bite her boob. She got cross. I think she was in large amounts of boob-specific pain. I felt bad. In Ulaanbaatar, I received a wordless email from her, with a photo of a pink-and-purple breast in the attachment. The subject line instructed me not to share it with anyone else.

Some minutes into the chant, my gray pony begins dancing his hooves. A giggle ricochets down my body. I turn him away and see Matthias splatted out on the ground. Above him stands his confused pony—*What little effort, for such results.* The lama in red chants on, unaware. To the rescue strides the British doctor assigned to monitor competitors. He picks his way through the ponies, moving to the glory of his bristling beard, and leans down to inspect the wilted Matthias, while the Scottish head vet marches in to catch the loose pony. It kicks him. He rebounds with a pained vowel, muffling his whelp so as not to interrupt the lama.

Twelve minutes of chanting quietens us, though most riders don't know quite what has been said—as far as I'm aware, none of us understands Tibetan. I have a verdant urge to explode into the plains. There's an umbrella planted at an angle ahead, absurd in the midmorning heat. If ultra-trained Matthias is already on the ground, I've no hope of making it beyond the horizon line. So I'll be the first past that umbrella and at least begin the race with a win.

"Shall we give o'er and drown?" says the Boatswain in *The Tempest*. "Have you a mind to sink?"

10 a.m.

Bang.

Katy, dressed in jeans and cowboy boots, fires a handgun and my pony—the only gray in the group—yawns into a rocking-horse canter. I hold myself in, absorbing the waves of his motion. "Choo choo!" I flick his shoulder twice. It's enough to shock him into a gallop. We reach the umbrella first. Delight.

We've cast away, movement wildly calming. Up the striding plain we go, in a group formed like a bicycle peloton. Riders shift between brisk trots and uncertain canters. The photographer bounces by, and I'm caught in a snap with Tom. My mother will make her disapproving face when she sees it. His sunglasses are thin and unfriendly; he drives his pony with the sobriety of a pilot.

My hues are mainly blue, jodhpurs being navy (sporting the name of Mum's jewelry business, Julia Lloyd George—my clothing sponsor) and vest being denim. The latter may prove me the teenager I suppose I still am. Lower down I've wrapped my calves in two pairs of half chaps to prevent the mango-sized welts Devan warned me about. On my head is Aunt Lucinda's lightweight riding helmet. She told me it would be too thin to protect me if I fell, but I was taken with the idea that it would absorb my forehead sweat.

When the film crew passes by in their jeeps, Monde, a horse-whisperer from South Africa, waves to them. Monde is the Derby's first black competitor, and some Mongolian families at the horse stations will line up for photos with him, not having met someone with dark skin before. I follow Monde's lead, gesturing and grinning to the film crew. Glee is my favorite train to catch; it really carries me. Soon I am letting out shrill hollers and woo-hoos.

Monde's employers had teamed up to pay for his race entry. Many others in our crowd had sponsors' logos pasted on their helmets. Others still were in immense debt, having had no luck with commercial support. As I rode that first leg, I questioned again why we were all willing to give up so much for a horse race. We seemed to have paid an extortionate amount to live out the idea of returning to a wilder time.

XIII

The jeeps disappear. Riders splay out into the unknown. My pony is slow. We fall from group to group until we're alone. He plods up a rise in the land, one hour in. I will call him "Brolly" after the leg, because of his speed to the umbrella at the start. "Gelatinous disc of a jellyfish" is the dictionary's fourth meaning for "umbrella," and Brolly now drifts in a jellyfish fashion, awaiting a current to carry us. Wild horses often move with the weather. With no coming storms to bluster his backside, Brolly and I fall so far behind I can't even see any dots of riders ahead.

Where to go? I was hoping to follow someone. Every minute I scan the horizon in search of the next station. I almost lose my balance taking in the transparent distances. I can see only sun. Her heat is swelling me, I feel I no longer fit inside my body.

Apparently the horse stations, or *urtuus*, are formed by two or three white gers and a horse line. Earlier in the summer the Derby's head horseman Unenburen Uyndenbat traveled the steppe with race organizers to ask families if they could bring thirty to forty ponies together to make an urtuu. Some families have as many as two hundred horses and can create a station singlehandedly; others team up with neighboring herders. On the days when the riders are expected to arrive, the selected ponies wait around the urtuu horse lines, and the families charge the organizers for each pony competitors ride.

As far as I can tell, there are no urtuus in sight. I'd imagined the medieval postal system the race re-creates as a series of stations spaced according to the contours of the country; I thought I might always be able to see the next station on the horizon.

From my denim vest pocket I unleash the one, the only, the cumbersome Garmin eTrex GPS: a thing like a mobile phone from the 1990s, coated in gray rubber with a small screen. I have been too scared to turn it on, in case my very touch tampers with its highly strung technological heart. Now it is blinking to life and rudely suggesting we're only a quarter of the way to the first station.

It must be past lunchtime when my pony and I head out of the plains towards a mountain range. Sweat is dribbling over my eyelids, and the cross-strap backpack is digging into my ribs. I have run out of water. My mouth is dry. I think of lancing Brolly's veins and drinking his blood, Mongol-warrior-style—Chinggis Khan and comrades rode horses to near-death on the campaign trail—but as we totter on, old Khan is forgotten. The medieval re-creation seems a farce. At the level of each beating hoof, this race superlatively long and tough might turn out to be chronically ordinary. We're just trotting a path through grass.

Brolly is thirsty too. The map book instructs us to seek water in wells, rivers, lakes, ponds, springs, and waterholes, none of which we've passed. I sneak a Sesame Snap from my pocket and munch in rhyme to Brolly's trot. Then I look at my watch again, five minutes since I last looked at it. Time becomes a tool for passing time itself.

As we curve each valley corner, we set the plains behind us free. Grasslands pull the summerscape in every direction. Green, green, gulping us up. Where the grass ceases, blue sky begins, translucent and bold. "Blue and green should not be seen, without a color in between," begins my mother, babbling in my head wherever I go. "Blue and green *should* be seen," she carries on, reminding me of the philosophy behind her jewelry making, which marries emeralds to sapphires at every opportunity.

Brolly, a young soul under old fur, is ever slower. *My, just a horse race, don't be silly.* Between each urtuu are roughly 40 kilometers, and I have no idea how far that really is. It will turn out to be neither here, nor here, nor there at the bottom of the page. It is nestled far outside this rectangle.

I rise up, I sit down. I rise up, I sit down. A thousand beats of trot and still the scenery won't shift. Nor are there any nooks or lonesome trees for me to chat to. As soon as I'm tempted to get upset, the undetailed land sits on my drama, as if to say, *I don't give a damn.* Brolly and I are mere passersby. A train of bad thoughts. He blows through his nose most beats. I snort in agreement. *Forgive me for asking, long girl, but would you allow someone to balance on your back in this manner?* God no. Rather die, I would. *Than be possessed like this?*

Well, I'm not sure I really like being aboard a horse, either. I can't believe it's taken all these years to hit me again—my original sentiment. It's visible in a photo of me age three on Costa, my cousin's Shetland pony. I should stare boldly over the pony's head—carefree niece of a champion—but my eyebrows are swept together in a frown. I want to return to the ground where my brothers stand, flanking Costa's shoulders. To be up here, in this pose, is strange and exhausting: legs strained, back stiff, knees hinged.

We enter a burnt valley, green grass paled to yellow, earth chapped and bare. A series of creases forms the unreachable hills ahead.

So this was how racing would be? A serious struggle, or perhaps an unserious struggle. If I did manage to finish, I was probably going to be last—nothing I minded when it came to exams, but I couldn't stand the idea of it in a race.

Apparently the matter in our bodies only makes up a tiny speck of dust. It has something to do with the distances between our atoms being so vast—as vast as the distances between urtuus.

To the people I wrote to before departure, pleading for charitable donations, I was exactly this, I suppose: a tiny speck among other bunched specks. I hated the idea that I could be seen now, even in minuscule form, as I rode. I wanted to purge myself from the radar. Was anyone I knew even looking at the tracking map? I'd told my charitable sponsors that 40 percent of riders never made it to the finish. Some of my parents' friends had taken the trouble to write encouraging notes like *I do hope you don't get a sore behind*.

As the hours rolled by, voices leaked in—the future's past-tense voices. What stories would they pluck from the skies if and when I disappeared from the map?

Her armpit hair grew too long.

She missed the plums and her father's blackened toast, his figure by the slowly roaring fridge.

My journey aboard the first horse climaxes when I enter a silent tantrum. Perhaps I believe this tantrum will offer escape. That it will transport me home, where I shall strip my wallpaper, sharpen all the pencils, and lavish myself in mundane things that could have been just as exciting as this race if only I'd used my imagination.

I can't be sure we're going the right way—the GPS is not clear, much less the landscape. I look about the valley and wonder where I'm headed, and indeed where my head is. How much of us is really moving forward if Brolly has already given up? After swinging south of the mountain range, the cat is truly out of the bag: he hates this. I get off and walk next to him.

At home, the pain of animals makes me shiver: when the dog whines after stealing too much salted butter or falls ill with testicle pain, or when my brother Arthur taunts me with "I'm going to put Hammy in the oven" and I shriek over the fictitious fate of my hamster. Now, at the center of a signless valley, I can offer no solution to the gray pony at my side.

As we go like treacle towards the hill, I relax out of my tantrum into a more bland potato state of mind. For some minutes, I relocate myself in June, back when I was looking forward to this race with such romantic ideas, of dancing ponies on blankets green, of dazzling scenes and legs so keen. I don't know which wise man coined the saying "Life begins outside your comfort zone," but Brolly and I have proven him wrong. Life, whatever that is, has gotten a wagonload worse. Stuck in a sludgy slow-motion, still walking at Brolly's side, I move with my usual stomachache and dull thoughts of a missed lunch. Quitting the expectation game, one horse at a time.

We're 2 kilometers from the station when a herder in a maroon cloak trots into our universe. He makes choppy gestures for me to remount, so I wing my legs back onto Brolly, whose eyes are now surrounded by gunk. The man leans over to whip my dear plod every stride. I see how his technique keeps Brolly trotting, and I question why I didn't use it too.

The urtuu ahead is formed on a lull of earth that rises to tumbling rock formations. A steppe town glistens on the heat-waved horizon. At the urtuu I will hand Brolly over to the vets for assessment. Because our leg has taken five hours, the other riders will be gone by the time we arrive.

Propped on a bank before the station is a Soviet-era camper van. An interpreter and a paramedic crouch at its wheels, hiding from the sun, perhaps thinking, *Yawn, here comes another rider*. I am just a piece of driftwood, floating down the stream.

"Am I the last?" I ask.

They're surprised I didn't know. "Yes, apart from Matthias."

XIV

Home time. Teatime. This must be more or less the finish line. Waiting for the vet, I breathe in the cheese scent of Brolly's goatskin bridle. There is something cozy about the smell of decay.

Seven riders are still at the urtuu waiting for their ponies' heart rates to drop. Time never ceases in the race—each minute waiting for a horse's heart is a minute wasted or savored: it depends on whether you prefer your legs apart or together. Yesterday Maggie the steward told me that most of the horses ridden in each Derby—nearly a thousand are gathered in its name—have heart rates that fall below 64 beats per minute within ten minutes, unless the weather is this kind of despicable sauna. Even Brolly, who stands before me having done so little, takes twelve minutes to go from 72 to 64 bpm.

I find a single bar of signal on my phone while waiting and use it to text the Mongol Derby blog. My message is only a sentence. It doesn't dare mention the race. Maybe that's because I feel the Derby might be an illusion and I want to exist beyond it. Instead, I complain about the plums ripening without me at home. Picking plums is one of only two moments in life in which I really feel at ease, the other being when I'm lost in the troughs of my yawns. Every year I involve myself in the plums' journeys from March to August—green to purple, hard to soft, healthy to diseased—their changing skins mapping the arc of each summer, their flesh tasting of sun and birthday and moments alone.

Tom hangs in a sweat nearby, his torn shoulder crumpled into his sling, his other arm draped over his steed's neck. Richard the photographer mills about, his gray hair striking upwards. I see Maggie fix her eyes on me. She orders Brolly to trot. I wake him up and we hop into rhythm.

"Your horse," she booms after ten strides, "is lame."

I wince. Lame? Limping and injured? My stomach recoils. I was a bit suspicious two hours ago when Richard drove back past in his jeep.

"He feels lame!" I'd yelled to him. "Does he look lame?"

"Looks fine."

To avoid a penalty we're supposed to dismount lame horses and walk them to the nearest station. I should never have gotten back on. Richard chips into Maggie's glare and decides my fate.

"No, no. T'sallright, Maggie. I passed them earlier. Pony was sound." His faint Irish accent unstiffens the consonants.

Maggie turns her attention elsewhere. Why she'll take the word of a photographer, I don't know. I untack the little gray—who will now have days, or even months, off. Bye-bye, Brolly.

In a few weeks' time I'll make an inventory of the ponies I've ridden, in case I forget any of them. *1: Umbrella/Brolly—Small. Gray. Lame.*

✦

After a certain number of days, straggling riders get kicked out of the race because the crew cannot monitor the field if it spreads out too much. I'll be the first cast-off if I don't get a move on. But where are the toilets? I'm looking for a complex similar to that of start camp. When a rider points me to a lone hole in the ground concealed by a flap of material, I decide I'll wait for the next station.

I stride up the horse line, a rope suspended between poles, and pause at each pony tied to the rope—brown, gray, spotted, black, then red. Which of these stumpy legs is willing? I'm seeking someone who will bolt me to the next station, but they all stand in sun-smothered slumbers, occasionally shaking their manes to throw off the flies. Before I left I asked my aunt if she had advice on picking a semiwild horse from a selection of up to forty. "Bloody hell, no," she replied.

Behind the lines, the herders are laughing. Maybe I look like an idiot, I don't know. When I point at a big brown pony with a red noseband, one man in a gray cloak cackles louder. I frown and turn to his son, whose smirk is just as strong. It seems they have secrets about my desired mount. I look back to the pony's eye.

The herders do know all sorts of things; for example, horses with pointy ears tend to have healthier kidneys, which is news to me. They may know of an affliction in this pony. Or they may be amused at the thought of a girl handling him. Some Mongolian writers say women are respected here (whatever that has ever meant), as they were during the medieval empire, when they exercised power— Töregene Khatun, the wife of Chinggis Khan's son, ruled as regent for five years—but perhaps they're not always so welcome on the horse-racing scene. There was only one girl among many boys in the short race we saw at start camp.

Though many people outside of Ulaanbaatar know how to ride, the warrior arts are reserved for men. Lucy, the past competitor

I spoke to on the phone, said herders, when asked, sometimes recommend slower horses to female riders out of concern for their safety. I leave the herders' lingering laughter and scoop up my saddle to lay it on the brown pony's back.

Saddles in England are traditionally leather and saddles in Mongolia are wood, but we're using nylon endurance saddles. We also have two girths to stop them from slipping around to the horses' underbellies, since a capsized rider is a classic equestrian accident.

When I return from refilling my collapsible water bottle, an English competitor in sunglasses shouts over to me.

"Wait for me while I go to the loo, yah?"

The vowels of her refined English accent resonate across the heat. At home I wouldn't have noticed her voice—it simply echoes mine—but out here I envisage a British flag and awful cries of *Empire! Empire!* or *War? Why not!*

Distance has a strange ability to make matters more acute. I'm uneasy about my Britishness, and its link to the quest for empire—a past long gone, but not gone yet, a past that feels, in this moment, to be one of its defining features.

The English competitor is visibly still at the toilet when I scribble my signature on the sign-out sheet. When a journalist publishes an article online about my attempt at the race, she writes it in my first-person voice, using tenuous quotes like *If someone is injured or in trouble of course I'll stop, but I don't plan to wait for anyone who can't find their gloves.* It makes me sound ruthless. I mean, it's true I don't wait for the English competitor, but she will find others to ride with—many at this urtuu are stagnant in the midday sun, still awaiting their horses' recoveries.

My other option is to hang around and continue alone in last position to satisfy the part of me that likes being slow and disaster-ridden. Aunt Lucinda still enters some competitions, but with a less good horse than those she used to ride, and never for a placing or a prize.

"Are you sure you want to compete at Blenheim to be bottom?" her half sister Karol asked her this year.

"Well, someone has to be bottom," she replied.

I think my tendency to be bottom is at odds with my urge to move—and no better animal with whom to move away than the horse, the queen of flight.

The brown pony canters me off into the waiting land ahead. By the hill we are bolting, up and up towards a curtain of sky. I fold my back low to the gallop, leaning parallel to the lightning beneath me. His power is pure as an idea. After plodding on Brolly, it's a relief to feel movement for the love of it. We go as one circuit: down my arms, into his head, back to his body, and up my legs as the mud flies from his hooves. I'm thankful there are no English village lawns to worry about mashing up.

Adam and Lynne, with whom I left the last station, keep the pace. Our twelve legs travel with the swiftness and intention of an invasion. I am certain, perhaps prematurely, that I lie in good hands. Adam is an American with well-sculpted features and dark hair. His horse is corkscrewing and tugging at his reins. Lynne is a Canadian businesswoman and mother of many. She sent me for my final shower yesterday since I had forgotten, as usual, to wash.

After half an hour, Lynne's pony shoots ahead into the valley below. Unnerved by her tension, he is taking her where he pleases. Adam and I go together awkwardly, but this doesn't stop me imagining riding the entire race with him, conducting a dreamy love affair along the way. I still have a schoolgirlish ability to fall for men, even, and especially, when they have shown no interest—not one friendly phrase nor any eye contact.

We rise over a pass and creep along the high ground of a new valley. Prehistoric stone slabs jut out from the slope, casting themselves in long shadows. We find bones scattered among them and I reckon I sniff violence lurking in the earth. Perhaps this was a battlefield. Or a burial site? It might be the graveyard of Chinggis Khan—no one knows where he lies. He asked that everyone on the path to his burial be executed, and a river be diverted over his grave. He was buried with his horses. No great tomb, no palace, no trace.

The pony and I are getting on well, though sadly the partnership with Adam is crumbling. In the dip of a hillock, he shouts at me to halt the canter. I turn. He's entangled in his backpack. I tell him he should not get off to disentangle. Our ponies want to gallop up a storm and can't be trusted.

"I will not be going to find your horse when it leaves us for China." I hear my crisp accent as I tell him this. It's not cool like his American one. My consonants are oh-so-entitled.

I mustn't be condescending to Adam. It might put our unfolding romance in peril. He submits nonetheless, making do with holding the tangled pack in one hand and his reins in the other. A certain kind of man aboard a horse is a funny sight for me, and such a man on a pony takes leave of comedy and enters the absurd. Ponies are strong enough to unseat even the muscliest of riders. It's a quiet threat that seems to unscrew manhood with every stride.

◆

We curve off the high ground and drop into an endless green valley, large enough to render us matterless. Clenched above my pony's bouncing trot, I turn to Adam. His bright-red gear is a quick reminder we're only pretenders. I'm certain he and I should have fallen atop one another in a bush by now, but instead he's dragging like a mop, backpack held to his belly. My turning gives him an excuse to begin again.

"Can we walk the horses now? This backpack is killing me."

I don't know how to respond.

At home in Britain, people tend to appreciate sulk, and rain, but only as a baseline drone, rarely as drama. Adam takes no measures to restrain his pained expression, as if he didn't choose to sign up for the race, but rather was borne into it as its victim.

We might be in pain, but we are not marooned at sea, or trying to live in the aftermath of an earthquake. The Derby's ten days will be so few among the year's three hundred and sixty-five. Do we not have this, a vague awareness of time?

I try to catch the giant, elastic journey and pull it back to just here, now, *clip clop clip clop*. For another hour we murmur along ridges rising into spindly rock turrets, and reach for ourselves down in the plains. This feels to me like some place across the river, across the boundary—not the middle of nowhere but the center of old dreams and unthought-of ideas.

The only gers we pass are piled with small white shapes, which are a mystery from a distance. As we near them the light lifts, revealing lumps of drying yogurt on the canvas roofs. Summer has brought in the animals, who in winter are too weak to be milked. Goat's milk, sheep's milk, cow's milk, yak's milk, and horse's milk are all being churned up by strong August arms. We ride only geldings and stallions, the male ponies, because the mares around here are reserved for milking and breeding (in parts of eastern Mongolia, herders do not milk the mares but ride them instead).

We're nestled into the leg when Lynne tumbles from the hills like a boulder. Adam heaves to another halt to redo his backpack and Lynne waits for him while I ride on with a group of riders we've caught up with. It's possible she needs these minutes to calm herself. Her office-conditioned fretfulness is not going down well with her pony. Like any horse, he lacks speech and makes up for it with his strengthened sensitivity to the unseen. Where humans might fail to grasp one another's inner workings, the feeling of rider anxiety is obvious to a horse.

Aunt Lucinda always talks about the horse's seventh sense (she says people have six), which knows our emotion before we do. The unity with a horse, the very idea of the centaur, is a unity of minds. When a human is tense, the horse will flee—flight is, after all, the horse's natural expression.

I cast aside my fantasy relationship with Adam and ride on with the new group through thick grasses. I am munching on my last Sesame Snap when Monde starts talking about "hanging right in the lowlands," which leads to an extended navigational debate.

The night before I left Ulaanbaatar, Mum and I had an email exchange about snacks and alterations to our home. *Everyone else is having light neutral colors all the same, then your explosion,* she wrote, objecting to the cockatoos I wanted to paint on my walls. This she followed with capital letters, which were unreal to me, since she rarely shouts. *DON'T EAT THE SESAME SNAPS SILLY BILLY NEED THEM FOR THE RIDE.*

But of course I had. Ate nearly all of them out of boredom before start camp.

After the debate, the pack splits. I follow two riders towards the mountains, going as the crow flies, which is the GPS's idea of a shortcut. Down the corridor of the land, storm clouds are approaching. Our bodies beckon them to refresh our reptilian skin. I lapse into passenger-seat mode while Kirsten, an Australian who fainted at the doctor's talk in Ulaanbaatar, does our navigating. She rises punchily to the trot while conferring with her GPS. I get the sense she's uninterested in chat. I myself am sore, and very much done with this day.

The sky will break soon, and there's no knowing where we'll bed down. My bungee rope is at hand, which could result in a lovely night. For years I've been dreaming of sleeping beside a horse. They say that in the first year of the race, riders expected to fend for themselves, so they packed tents and stoves, clueless as to what lay ahead. How sad they didn't know about my lightweight, tentless option. Starry nights tied to a horse's tummy, lying down on soft grass. And as far as I'm concerned, there is only grass. Wolves, snakes, and mountain lions can't eat me because I'm not yet aware they roam these parts.

The air is raw and wet. Kirsten slides off to don a rain jacket. There are no keys to this race, but Lucy did say never to get off the ponies between urtuus, unless they're lame. Horses' eyes miss nothing. The slightest crinkle of our rain jackets, and they'll shudder, spook, and ping away. "The sooner you recognize you look like a hazard to them, the better," Maggie had explained.

Without ado, Kirsten climbs back on. Her pony chuckles at me, too interested in his grass to sprint away. It darkens at 7 p.m. Thunder burgles the sky as we sweep up off the plains. When lightning vaults and releases indigo rain, I feel as though we've ridden into a washing machine. Ten seconds and I'm wet at the undersides of my skin. Hail arrives and pelts the horses. Mine tenses his canter and stiffens his ears as he advances through the ice bullets. I am pitched over his body like a tent in the wind.

We move into pixelated vision up the valley, whose dark-clouded end will lead to another earth. The only man-made furniture in sight is a lone barn. We head towards it, but the hail only pounds louder under its tin roof. The body beneath me cowers inside his coat heavy with water. I stroke his neck as we stare out into rain—and then we ride on, curling ourselves against the teeth of the storm.

In the gulley behind the barn the ponies push their way through a barricade of giant stinging nettles, which reach through my jodhpurs to sting my thighs. They startle the pony, too. His back rocks in the walk.

When the hail recedes, Kirsten and Sandra, a ringletted blonde from France, huddle for discussion. I stand apart, superfluous. My best guess is we've been conjured into the beyond, untraceable. But there's the flash, flash, flash of the satellite tracker on my chest, shipping our signals off every minute. It even has an SOS button for calling the paramedic, who's apparently never more than a five-hour drive away. Via satellite telephones, the paramedic and crew receive our coordinates from headquarters in Ulaanbaatar. So we may be hidden, but there is mighty trace. I understand the organizers have chosen these mitigations because they don't want us to die on the Derby. After all, we have paid to turn wild, and everyone would like us to return to tell the story.

I have a fear of being traceable. If others don't have information about me, I feel more powerful, more free. I know that not being accompanied by their phone is, for some people, akin to leaving their mouth at home, but I would like to toss mine into a stream and leave it to live as a pebble.

Cantering out of the rain, I'm desperate for a wee. But I won't get off because what if the pony vanishes behind my back? Two valleys over, we reach a peak surrounded by hills smiling through rainlight. A musky post-storm air drifts with a highland scent. Mist rises from the scattered rocks. We come to an *ovoo*, a shrine created with a pile of stones—this one wound with blue scarves in honor of the peak and of *tenger*, the sky. Shatra, a Derby organizer who lives between Hawai'i and Ulaanbaatar, says that in the old days, people would make ovoos to mark their journeys or places they had lived, Sometimes too, they would make an *ovoo* to warn others about dangerous areas.

Passersby are meant to add a rock to the ovoo in respect and then circle it three times clockwise to bless their journey. This shamanic practice predates Buddhism in Mongolia by thousands of years. I have been told that even secular Mongolians from the city still tend to flick milk to the heavens and place stones on ovoos. Shamans, meanwhile, are central to many steppe communities. Among other business, they maintain relations with nature and hold ceremonies to heal people, often by retrieving their souls.

Under communist rule, both Buddhist and shamanic worship were forbidden in Mongolia, but the steppe was unyielding to the Ulaanbaatar government, and devotion to ovoos continued in secret. I'm pleased by the thought of this spot free from the outstretched tentacles of the city authorities. I sing as we circle the rocks and scarves while Kirsten records on her camera. She shouts after us as we stride off into the evening. "Your singing voice could injure a small child."

In old Mongolian folklore, weather is a manifestation of Tengri the sky god's mood, lightning a sign of his power. My clothes will not dry as the cold air of night settles, but having made it through the storm, I forget the idea that there's more to come. In *The Tempest*, the opening sea-storm unhinges human government, washing characters onto the island's shore. There, cleansed by the squall, they seem fresher than before. The steppe downpour has christened me into my journey. I feel horrible yet whole.

Seduced by the sway of the animal beneath me, I begin daydreaming. For some minutes, I imagine seals, envious that they can spend nights on beaches without getting cold. Then again, they do exhibit a striking lack of athleticism as they balloon over rocks. Would I sacrifice my ability to move on land for the talent of sleeping at peace on it, at the edges? These thoughts I raise with Kirsten and Sandra, and their reply is silence.

We ride on through a symphony of green. The hills cushion our sides, ushering us on.

XV

The evening is clouding herself together. The second urtuu lies in view up the hill. The bungee rope lets out a forlorn moan from inside my backpack. *Tomorrow night*, I say, *your turn will come*. We have until 8:30 p.m. to make it to the urtuu, after which we'll be penalized with a two-minute wait for every minute over. We come to a stream around 8 p.m.

> But the majestic river floated on,
> Out of the mist and hum of that low land.

These lines from Matthew Arnold's *Sohrab and Rustum* doze in my Winnie-the-Pooh notebook, mirroring the Mongolscape. Wide-eyed Iona, a friend of Arthur's, sent me a list of poems the night before I left Ulaanbaatar, this one from Macaulay:

> To every man upon this earth,
> Death cometh soon or late.
> And how can man die better
> Than facing fearful odds . . . ?

She hoped the poems would be my solace, but they left me with a grand sense that I was embarking on a mission for a higher cause. *Which you are so ploddingly not*, utters the pony beneath me.

When we reach the urtuu at 8:15 p.m., Helen the vet, a jovial South African, greets us in an oversize raincoat. Her nimble, blue-eyed face and wispy blond hair remind me of my mother. She bends to the pony, listens to his heart, and announces that its rate is well below 64. I ask the interpreter to thank the herder for allowing me to ride this creature. I want to speak Mongolian directly to him, and it feels shameful that I can't. Is it a crime to grin at him instead? We humans speak ten thousand languages; a little eye contact must ripple through them all.

Devan Horn was well into the lead.

"At least four hours ahead of you guys," said Gloria, the ABC reporter with real-life airbrushed cheeks.

Apparently Richard was with Devan at urtuu 3, snapping photos of her lying imperially upon a bed.

I bent through the doorframe of a ger and fumbled over some sleeping bodies. The more awake riders were discussing the news: Devan had managed three stations when the rest of us had barely done two. Matthias was down and out—that was a shock—but the Texan's race was going according to her plan, with the bonus of a bed.

That night, the Mongol Derby website published an interview with the race's founder. Who, he was asked, will win?

"I haven't a clue," he said, pausing. "Time and a thousand kilometers of arse-pounding steppe will tell."

In horse riding sports, competitors often don't invest in winning. You go out in the simple hope that you and the horse will get on well together over the obstacles at hand. Maybe Devan's attitude added an Olympic tinge to the Derby that year, one from which her fellow competitors, including me, were failing to find immunity. Few riders had taken the race so seriously in the past, when pairs shared first place, men crossed the finish line holding hands, and riders drank spirits while racing.

I slide about camp, skirting clusters of people and their conversations. I have an appointment with the evening and don't want to be noticed. When I see someone turn, I dart into the crowded ger, where a broad-cheeked lady from the urtuu's Erdenebileg family sets hot noodle-and-mutton soup on my lap. Five gulps, finished. Dotingly she passes me a second helping. I thank her endlessly, meaninglessly, and withdraw to a corner to strip off my soaking jodhpurs. Next to me a rider is pinning herself into yogic positions, "easing the tension," she says, twisting her head away from me. I sit scratching my legs.

Half an hour past the 8:30 deadline, businesswoman Lynne rides in with a sad story on her lips. After she fell behind Adam, a drunken man chased her on his motorcycle, groped her, and tried to lasso her pony.

Once everyone is tented, I twirl and sprint and go, horseless down the wet, grassy hill and up again. Noodle energy. My feet flap along under the mass of me, yelping. The bunions are cross after their full day in boots. I return panting to a girl who shows me the toilet, which is simply earth, all earth. You can go anywhere. I crouch to the earwigs, who graze the evening in search of lost centuries. Fading rain and final sunlight dab the hills around this, the coziest of valleys. Lying between here and the finish is twelve times today's distance. My, how many days will that take?

Deep in our sleeping bags, Natacha and I marvel at how strange it is not to have seen each other since the start line. Already time is passing strangely, and the morning feels a billion years behind us.

When I mention I might ride with her tomorrow, Natacha replies, "No bloody way am I riding with you! I don't trust you one *inch*." She lands on the "inch" and splutters onwards, as though coughing the idea of me out of her system. "Can you imagine how wrong things would go! You'd get me so lost we might even disappear from this earth."

I cackle, mildly offended, wondering whom I will ride with instead since there's no chance I'll find my way alone.

I didn't think about rain, so I don't have a change of clothes. No pajamas. No second pair of jodhpurs. Just a spare pair of socks and a pair of knickers. "Oh dear, I'm going to have to sleep naked."

It wasn't necessary for me to say that aloud but I don't think anyone noticed. At the end of a day on a horse, you can bed down anywhere, in any company. I jot some notes into Winnie-the-Pooh—*First pony a tortoise and a hare. Won the umbrella race then lost his legs. Such a jolly long-john's way*—and peel off my wet underwear, hugging my knees to squeeze out the cold.

Dear Mum,
I'm trying to fall asleep, imagining the parts you've played in this story, since its beginnings lie

not now, but with you. Brolly, my first pony of the Derby, was just like Brendon, with similar gray fur and balky behavior.

This race is not an arrow shooting out of a bow. We pause at the stations and cease in the evenings. If an arrow at all, it stutters a lot and would like to return to its bow. Perched in this Elysian valley among snoozing people from faraway lands, I ask myself if we're even racing.

I'm not sure how aware you are of my habit of moving away, but it's one I tend to lapse into, especially when bodies are stuffed together in social gatherings. It always feels to me as if we're a bubbling liquor, or a waiting violence. I can't cope with the desire for climax and the simultaneous going-nowhere-ness, so I flee, or estrange myself in daydreams.

Things are different in this tent. Our gang is intent on racing and sleeping rather than stirring up social potions. We form a harmless, haphazard collection, only accidentally social. I'm spinning out a love affair with the oddity of our day together. I've been flinging remarks at Todd, the Australian snoozing beside me who told someone at start camp to "just hurry up" and sleep with him. I can see the outline of his smile, but he isn't replying. This may mean I'm ruining his dreams of beer. Am resisting the urge to tug at his beard. If you were here you might call me an annoying bluebottle.

Today, Ma, I have seen the earth thrusting storms around and pulling bones down to her core. The coldness has left me aching and broken, like eggshell. It's useful pretending I'm neither cold nor achy, thinking of seals and such like, but then I wonder whether it's helpful to always be an actor to myself, as though this isn't painful—or as though the wound inside my tummy isn't there. Am I a stranger to my deepest depths? How do we all lock so much inside our eyes?

Itching rules the night. I pray nobody makes off with my jodhpurs before I wake.

I suppose it's not right, but I felt I was missing out when I was eleven. I swayed on the riding-school ponies like a shaking minaret and thought this meant I could ride, but I didn't have my own pony with whom to progress. I'd lie in bed in London, gazing at magazine adverts of competition ponies leaping over hedges, longing for that freedom and independence, plus the accompanying poo-picking rituals. But I feared Mum would go silent or judge me for daring to want such a Big Thing. It had taken at least a year of diplomacy to win her over with my hamster campaign.

Indeed, all the advertised ponies were too expensive, and my mother was hesitant—until I walked into the kitchen one July afternoon to find her in a state of ecstasy. What was it? Nothing other than the kitchen mice and the decoration of the Christmas tree ever propelled her into such hysteria. She told me how the vicar's wife's sister had put her in touch with an Irish lady selling a horse called Grageelagh Brendon. Word of mouth is my mother's trusty friend. She hadn't understood many details from Mary, Brendon's owner, on the phone, but she kept repeating one of Mary's lines in her attempted Irish accent—"Ooo, 'e'll do the job"—and thrust me a faxed photo of a jumping horse that may or may not have been Brendon. She had fallen in love with a hazy silhouette.

Mum knew he was only four, too young for an eleven-year-old's first pony, but how irresistible a price. Three days later I laid my head on her red poncho aboard the 3 a.m. ferry to Ireland. What with the stench, the sticky floors, and the noisy drunken men, we couldn't waste the journey. Brendon was already ours.

It didn't matter that we found him moping at the back of a dim stable in a crumbling yard run by loud chickens and a solitary goat, nor that Mary made jokes about the fact that I couldn't ride at all like Aunt Lucinda. Even now Mum hasn't forgotten the lunch of white bread and ham we were served, a meal she'd have stuck her nose up at in England but now, on an empty stomach in such a setting, found quite exquisite.

Brendon came home to Appleshaw. I flung myself into the relationship, devoted to the bum he so loved to thrust at me in the yellow stable. We often tried to take him cross-country jumping, Aunt Lucinda's forte, but he was rarely persuaded to step over the foot-high wooden carrot, let alone anything larger. His despondence made us feel hopeless, yet we were also hopeful and, somewhere, satisfied. *Early days.*

At the time, Aunt Lucinda was our comic engine, our oracle. As the winter light withdrew on Sunday afternoons, she'd sit in our kitchen advising, talking at the speed of a gallop with her lower back slumped, fidgeting as usual (she often picks at food just to give her hands somewhere to go, and has been known, as a guest, to consume a pot of honey at breakfast). Lucinda's rants would conclude with a "Crack on!" and leave us steaming with her energy, itself of military origin—her father, my paternal grandfather, whom neither my mother nor I have ever met, had commanded a cavalry unit. *Our family has always tried never to look back, only forward,* Lucinda wrote when he died in 1977, as though the Prior-Palmers had a constitution.

It was my grandfather who had begun the Appleshaw tack room, where his bits—the molded pieces of metal a horse takes in her mouth to receive direction—still hang like ammo, albeit beneath the spider webs that also shroud memorabilia from Lucinda's career: rotting horse wreaths, stable plaques from Badminton, a moldy "Welcome Home, World Champion" sign above the doorway. Though these objects were decaying by the time Brendon and I got to know them, their stories found life in my mind.

I am no longer sure that following in footsteps is a good aim, since a story can really only happen once in a family. It feels tiring enough inheriting some of their traditions; I often ask myself if I move through the world inside an envelope of the family declensions—blind drive and courage, critical vision and imperial self-importance—to name a few.

But in those early years, all I wanted was to ride at Badminton Horse Trials—the world's most challenging three-day event— where Lucinda had won age nineteen. I read all three of her books and dreamed of her beginnings, especially of Be Fair, her first horse, who'd made her European champion and was buried beside an Appleshaw compost heap which you could smell burning every autumn. My mother chimed in with nostalgic memories of Lucinda's competing days—the grace of her cross-country riding, her lemon-yellow colors, the tears of her supporters.

Mum herself was ant-like in her devotion to my cause, quietly present. She would arise on frozen winter dawns beneath her lopsided turquoise hat and drive me to fixtures across the West Country. Unmoved by the mothers who bought their children expensive horses for the national teams, she never saw the need for me to be mounted on anything more than an honest donkey.

And maybe the type of horse didn't matter to me, either. In one sense, those days were precious for the space they created away from home.

XVI

This morning the wakeup is successful, as far as wake-ups go—for I am still a teenager during this race, and waking up is not for fun. I have a theory, unproven, that the blood vessels in your eyes can burst if you get up too quickly.

I see figures clambering round the ger, organizing the dawn. Insect bites line my thigh and the nettle rash is in full bloom. I scratch hard, as if there's a herd of creatures to dig out from beneath my skin. I shouldn't have slept naked.

My socks have disappeared, the socks know where they are—these are the only words I write in Winnie-the-Pooh this morning. Slowly goes the hour. I pull my damp jodhpurs on and feel my buttock muscles losing the strength they regained in the night.

Without a shower to wash off my dreams, I push my head out into the tightness of morning. Raindrops tap at my ears. The long day will not hold my hand, but it feels created, and only created days can I seize. Creation was never the feeling when waking up in London to a thrash of cold water and Mum growling my name, white walls filling the daylight, uptight chimneys and dutiful pigeons holding the charade together outside the window.

Riders are leaving the urtuu. They rode in before me last night so they had first choice of the ponies at 7 a.m. I'm unsure what the time is now—the supermarket watch might have known, back when it was working properly. Glum horses face away from us on the line. They droop their eyelids, cock their back legs, and hang their heads low. Closer, I catch their warm, dirty smell as it steams up into the rain—horse-smell is the same the world over. I let it replace the absent breakfast.

There is something of a traffic jam at the lines, but eventually I get to choose a small dun. He's the color of darkening desert. The pixie inside me wakes a little after I do, when Alex from ABC asks for an interview while I tack up the horse.

"Looora, why do you always smile? Why do you always look so happy? Is that your strategy?"

I catch his eye across the pony's neck, laughing as the final words stream from his mouth, wondering how this slick, articulate man from Manhattan wound up here. His combed dark hair is clear-cut against the tangled horses' manes behind him.

"Strategy?" I say, looking away. "I'm not sure what that means. It's just easier to be happy when everyone's whingeing."

I mean to say, *I just love the situation!* But that sounds flippant, which is what happens when I try an American accent.

I'm not the happy-go-lucky deluxe edition Alex sees. I'm a natural grump who runs up to her bedroom to feast on forgettable fights with her brothers. But my smile today is true. Spirits are high.

The question is, what will I do when there's no one left to display jolliness to? I suspect I will cease being jolly.

Alex carries on with his questions. I chat to his camera as I move about the pony, fixing straps and girths into place. I can hear the doctor giving an intense interview to Gloria's camera beside me.

"You know, yesterday's riding encapsulated the extremes these riders are dealing with." He grunt-coughs and clears his throat, as if to boost his presence. "Just take a look at the thirty-two-degree heat and then the transition to the thunderstorm."

Damn, the reporters must like his stubble, his sensationalism, and his oracular sense of self. He will definitely make it onto the documentary instead of me. I don't know when that kind of British self-assurance became so marketable. Perhaps it's a good thing to be assertive. I'm just so used to swallowing myself as I speak that I can't help seeing self-assuredness as indulgent.

Good morning, sighs the crab-like pony. *Not going to climb onto my back are you. You?*

I swing aboard. We scuttle away; the urtuu melts into the hinterfog. Ahead is a sunken valley suspended in mist. As we bend our path to avoid it, the fog thickens. We can only see a few meters ahead—land and air morphed together. I take the GPS out of my pocket for a consultation. Despite doubting what I see and think, I tell Sandra and Kirsten it might be best to turn around. After the detour, they agree. I hope they're too navigationally stressed to notice that the recommendation came from me, the young one. There is something set apart about them—or is it me? It might be me.

My stomach moans in search of breakfast—*breakfast is not for fun, breakfast is expected.*

No, I say, don't you remember complimentary breakfast in the Ulaanbaatar hotel, where you ate everything and excused yourself because you needed to fatten up for the race?

It is true I ate the waffles, the pancakes, the carrot cake, the coco pops, the omelets, the toast, the fruit and the yogurt, the fried rice, the seaweed, and perhaps more. I say "perhaps" more because by this point I was so drunk on food that we—you and I—don't remember what happened next.

Crinkles of the human night are smoothed out as the pony trots beneath me, neighing occasionally, moving me always, filling me up. What is it that horses can do for us? It took years around them for me to feel the good ache, the warmth of these creatures so feared by my father.

Horse lovers, he might grumble, have *excessive* feeling.

Some of his favorite topics include the heating and burglars, the latter arousing such interest that he can talk about them at length—how often they come, what they do when they arrive, and when we can next be expecting them. Sometimes he examines the dog's larger poos on his lawn and decides human intruders have been plotting an attack all night. Every evening, he shuts every shutter, *bang-ba-bang bang-bang.* Maybe he is gratified by the idea that his home is worthy of burglary. Like a nation, he cherishes threat.

What is it that horses can do to us?

His sister, Aunt Lucinda, takes another angle. Recently she wrote of the "explosion of mental illness" in our age, "caused by many elements, not least of which is the dramatic speed with which life and communication have evolved within a single generation. In this context, horses have not changed and their heartbeat and ancient affiliation with man become a steadying, rooting influence to all of us involved with them."

Are you sitting comfortably? I am not—jog-jog-jog-jog-jogging. The ponies are slow, our rate is 8 kilometers an hour. Sandra's horse keeps tripping and she's getting catty with him in French. Anger vibrates through her locked-up chin, dyeing the air around her red.

Soon we move in a large group we might call the Fun Bus—a group of riders known to solidify every year somewhere in the middle of the pack, who generally have a good time in the company of others. I can't work out if I'm here to have a good time, nor whether this race could ever be a "good time."

My efforts at conversation are fruitless. Chat that might hold the ears at a dinner party is trampled under dutiful hooves, each rider vying to get ahead, too tired or pained to talk. Horses materialize from the fog behind and ahead. Natacha and her cavalier, middle-aged racing friend overtake us at a gallop and disappear into a white haze up the hill. She will ride the whole race alongside him, and he will get her a room in his five-star hotel when they return to Ulaanbaatar.

Kirsten and I keep our ponies trotting constant as the rain. The monotony of riding 40 kilometers settles early. I mow up my time filming riders on the flip-open device ABC Alex has lent me. The cameras are meant for the American riders, but he seems to have branched out. Maybe I bounded up to him for one too many interviews at start camp. I must've failed to contain my friendliness.

"Do you see that dot in the distance? That is Sandra. She's stuck in a heffalump trap, and I don't believe we'll be seeing her or her pony for many days now."

My commentaries are all false, and the pictures unsteady—

filmed by one shaky hand on the going pony. Kirsten and Sandra may view my filming as a distraction from the matter at hand, but the finish is so distant it almost seems behind us, hence I've got to make this bit now worthwhile. I do also like the thought of Alex watching these films in some lush city apartment in the future, asking himself whether it was all real. Last night his fellow producer even suggested I visit Alex when he next comes to England—as though I can begin making plans beyond this race. I suppose the idea of leaving always does assume a return, but here in the fog, a home-going seems further off than deep-ocean squid.

For an hour we trundle along. We're only jolts of motion-in-the-making, but when the grafting lapses into the past, there appears a gliding trail behind us, as though we didn't exert ourselves to get where we are, as though the earth is water and we have been fish, until now.

The rain comes in such lashings that I half close my eyes and so does the pony. I feel his rib cage judder as he whinnies at a passing herd, which makes me realize he probably has better things to do, but I'm talking to the rider in front of me so the thought cannot grow.

Ask again—what is it that horses can do for us?—and still I myself can't give a precise answer. When I arrive at a horse's side, I'm amazed I ever managed to forget that they in themselves could be my destination. I feel calm.

The horse has been sacred in many cultures for longer than I can know. Down the centuries, across Britain, people have created at least sixteen massive carvings of horses, eight of which are in Wiltshire. I could never fathom their size, nor understand their power, when I looked at them from the car as a child.

In Mongolia, there are, apparently, more love songs about

horses than about women. Ponies who come last in races are sung commiseration songs because no one wants them to feel bad. There's a sense in which your horse is an extension of you: *A Mongol without a horse is like a bird without wings*—so goes the proverb. Even horses' skulls are sacred. They're made into musical instruments, whose sounds comfort mourning souls.

The idea of the race recedes as the fog thickens. The disorientation makes me feel snug, as though I'm in one of those medieval paintings that's more than two-dimensional but not quite 3D, the scene curling around you. I trot into barren foothills on the trail of two English competitors, who believe, for quite a long time, that we are lost. Fogged out of existence. Occasionally we bump into twisted animal carcasses, whose dead peace I try to ignore.

I have given up on my Generally Purposeless Soulmate and lapsed back into reliance on those around me. It brays in my pocket. The English riders, Georgie and James, are mostly silent as they guide me along, occasionally conferring with each other as to the location of our lonely ridge in relation to the rest of the planet. I stalked them online before the race—they're twins my age; they have a Mongol Derby campaign website and everything. James wears a GoPro on his helmet, which makes him look a bit like a Teletubby.

We relax when we find ourselves, though the twins are soon uncertain again, speculating that these are the sinking sands the map book tells us to avoid. The dunes call for a slow march. We rest our reins and let the giggles rise from our new gang led by some South African riders who've flapjacked out of nowhere.

Despite the desert, it rains. They said the route to the finish would push us through fourteen different microclimates, so Devan, at least 50 kilometers ahead, is probably bathing herself in sunlight while we brace our faces against the rain and shiver. "You're not made of sugar—you won't melt," Mrs. Nunes used to tell us, back when we were twig-shaped children in her soaked school playground.

It's 104 degrees down in the actual desert at this time of year. The race's course won't traverse the Gobi region because the horses cannot tolerate the heat—people who live there tend to use camels for travel instead. They also use camels to guard their homes when they're away, and there's a story about a man who went to visit his neighbor and got sat on by his camel. This is told without humor because it is true.

Apparently the scale of the Gobi region is good for children's eyes. It stretches their sight and stops them from needing glasses. In the 1930s, an old lady in the Gobi told an Austrian visitor to take her gift of a lamp, "for his young eyes did not see as well in the desert night as her old ones."

The dunes fall away at a river. I cross upstream from the twins. A barking dog bounds out to munch the pony and me on the other side. You're meant to shout "Hold the dogs" at unknown gers, but this phrase wasn't on the syllabus when the lawyer who cycled over 6,000 kilometers to get here taught us Mongolian at start camp. Natacha and I sat below her bed mouthing *bayarlalaa* (thank you) and *khurdan* (fast). A khurdan horse, khurdan, bayarlalaa.

Two more dogs dash over and snap at the pony's hind legs. He slows again. I ask for a gallop, but he can't hear. His trot is sideways, his lust for life surrendered. The original dog stands back and barks. Damn that rabies vaccine. If I fall now, what will happen? They say even Chinggis Khan was scared of dogs, though his armies traveled with any number of them, using them as sentries and in attacks.

The thirteenth-century Mongol ruler is very alive in our minds, but like all dead men he's mostly imagined, bound by myth. No one knows if that's true—about the dogs. It comes from *The Secret History of the Mongols*, the main document chronicling Chinggis Khan's life. It's full of persuasive reports—the great leader, they say, was born clutching a giant clot of blood on the Onon River.

We edge forward. All three dogs cease nipping and focus on barking. This must be the invisible camp perimeter. Through some internal logic, my pony decides we're safe and bursts into a gallop. We speed down the banks to catch the others, his sandalwood coat rippling over his braced muscles.

"Do you see blood on his back legs?"

Georgie inspects, finding nothing.

XVII

Welcome to the toilet, a stinking hole in the ground with wet boards above to stop you slipping into it. I like the absence of a seat—they can be so cold—but when I bend down, the pain of holding my body in this position is too much. With no celebratory flush to conclude, the quiet remains as I run back towards the horse lines. I hear laughter from two men of the Zangiat family who live at this urtuu. Should I not be running?

Urtuu 3 is set by river tributaries on a flood plain. With the fog lifted, the weather's better, but the puddles at our ankles contain memories of lengthy rain. Georgie has been standing perpendicular to her pony's wet chest since she arrived. She seems to have brought her own stethoscope. The secret to racking up 5 kilograms of luggage herein revealed: pack veterinary tools, proceed to entertain yourself at stations. The stethoscope will help her avoid a potential penalty by not "checking in" until her pony is cool.

I hop into a ger, tripping on the sacred entrance board. The woman of the place stares at me and I return her look. *Those legs are nothing to do with me, ma'am.* She hands me a bowl of soup, which has globules of mutton fat floating on the surface, and watches me eat. I say thank you, "bayarlalaa, bayarlalaa, bayarlalaa," perhaps too many times, perhaps not once comprehensible. Is this why Brits travel afar? To register their embarrassment in a more profound place? I turn and lift my head out of the ger to Georgie. She waits on the torn grass. Her pony's rib cage is still pulsating.

Sinking into the middle of the day, I do not feel bold so much as forced into boldness. Georgie is being held at the urtuu and Kirsten is out of sight. I herald myself onto a chestnut pony of no consequence and, with no idea where to go, I teeter away from the urtuu hoping space will piece itself together.

About fifteen minutes beyond the station, on some gummy mud between two valleys, messages begin to pass from his skin to mine.

What is this? I say.

The world in the raw.

What's "world"?

Well, precisely, he says.

I clutch at what might lie around the corner, how the land will bend this way and that, the future a curve I can't access. I think back to when I spied the landscape from the airplane window and felt I'd grasped it, yet that was nothing but an abstract sight. A map cannot lead a mind across a river.

The Derby organizers inscribed the race route onto Google satellite images and used them to compile the map book. It's not as confusing as the GPS, but it's still confusing, and blurry now, since the rain has sent the color running. Other riders seem to have waterproof jackets for theirs.

I relax at the sight of Kirsten edging towards me, but she can't decide where to go either. Dithering in company is nonetheless better than dithering alone. God forbid I'm ever left to navigate by myself.

"Kirsten, it's your decision," says I, the pompous English teenager, staring loftily into the sky.

"This way!" she shouts, trotting off.

"But this is northwest! They told us not to head this way." I imagine the area holds a biblical flood; Charles the steward told us to avoid it.

"Oh," she says.

We depart the tracks to canter after a herder, the only idea in sight.

"*Birrrrrd soum?*" I say, interrupting his day.

Kirsten chips in, "*Beeerrd soum?*"

The *soum*—which is to say, the town—of Burd is meant to be en route to the next station. We offer more variations, trying to straighten out our pronunciation.

"Burd," says the herder, unamused, as though we are neither friends nor aliens. Neutral non-relations.

"Yes! Yes, Burd," we chirp.

He points to what seems like a valley end and trots on with an enviable certainty about his day. We should've asked him how long it will take to get there, but forecasting journey times is bad luck. I have written the Mongolian for "How far is it?" in my map book, and though the first word is soaked, something like *kher khol vē* remains. If the race begins to madden me I will show the words to anyone I pass—how far is it? And they might reply, What's "it"—your infinite tomorrow?

The herder's suggestion is not the direction of the next station, so we ride back and forth undecided. A little time passes, and then a lot more. I feel a layer of distant frustration settle on my tiredness.

Yet neither Kirsten nor I exhibit signs of stress. I think the slung-out plains are moving us away from time.

The same herder rides back with a full storm of mares and foals in his wake. *What are you doing, loafing about the steppe?* Maybe he thinks this, maybe he does not. Maybe his mind is too large for our presence to surprise it. We decide, finally, to go his way. My legs are still damp from the morning's rain.

Water runs through the plain. We watch it charging. Neither of the ponies will cross so we stumble on through the floodlands, letting the river push us elsewhere until Kirsten gets fed up at a kink and takes an unannounced turn for the water. I feel my awe gathering until her submerging pony topples, taking her with him. There follows a mass kicking of legs. My admiration shifts to horror. Kirsten's pony heaves to land and points his ears backwards in search of her body, which is mainly beneath the murky surface. We must not mistake his behavior as loyalty—I think he merely lacks the oomph to gallop away from her through the swamp.

Out she clambers, roaring with laughter, firing off swear words with aspects of Australian slang. She leaps onto her dripping pony. I'm weak with laughter, though karma lets rip farther upstream when a bog traps my chestnut pony and my legs sink into peaty water. The chestnut struggles and I sit tense, clasping my legs, nothing to be done as he works his way out. Kirsten is again in fits of laughter.

On we wind up the wrong side of the river, the splash and suck of hooves filling the silent prairie. Soon there's a shape carving under the hill like the tip of a slow-breaking wave, closer, closer, until we guess it's Georgie, looking as directionless as we feel. From afar her whole being seems to twiddle its thumb. I suppose none of us can hope to appear intentional aboard struggling ponies against a rising hinterland. I wonder what she's doing here, and ask the same of my own un-thought-through presence, this body plonked on a plain away from home.

My, I didn't mean to get so serious in the middle of the day. It's that feeling of losing touch with the thicker points of dawn and dusk, no high stars or rising sun to cling to.

Across the river, Kirsten and I merged with Georgie and wound our ponies through slabs of rock. At no point in particular, Kirsten got off for a really long wee and I felt pangs of envy. I love a wild wee. It was dank around us and the clouds had piled high as if lining up for a funeral. We paused for the obligatory disagreement over direction, during which I sat in a daze and the ponies nattered. I didn't want to involve my GPS in the argument. It was enough for me to be participating in the race; I couldn't manage group-work too. I'd start making up what I thought.

"We need to cross over to that side of the valley!" So went Georgie's prim voice.

"Nah, nah," said Kirsten. "I'm staying over here." She gave her horse a convincing kick as the end of her sentence rose.

I followed Georgie, who had discarded her twin brother somewhere in the sands. She bounced along in her saddle at the trot, which likely saved her knees and ankles from swelling but it also meant her weight fell on her horse's back every stride.

After some minutes of following, I sidled up to her horse's shoulder.

"So has everyone overtaken us?"

The Fun Bus must have gotten past us in our hour of incompetence.

"Don't think so. I haven't seen any other competitors."

I let out a silent sigh.

Barks were echoing up the valley. Fanged watchdogs bounded out ready to devour us. Our horses cowered. I watched the snapping jaws with a little more love that time, knowing they didn't quite mean it.

Reports were filtering through headquarters in Ulaanbaatar. Devan Horn was 60 kilometers ahead of us—five hours' worth of riding. She had passed through urtuu 5, where she did not stop to eat. The vet was *impressed* by Devan's progress; the field should *be afraid, very afraid,* said Twitter, in the tone of a Hollywood horror. I was glad to be away from the incremental time of Twitter and other technologies.

I thought rarely of Devan. She was too far ahead to bother me at this point. The mass of my thoughts were only half formed and too dull for recording. As Georgie, Kirsten, and I rode the shoulder of a plain, a trio once more, I did have one question nagging me.

"Has it crossed anyone's mind what position we might be in right now?"

At my last count, I'd been in twenty-ninth place with Brolly, so anything twenty-eighth or upwards would be a relief.

"Yeah," replied Kirsten and Georgie in chorus. "We're fourth, fifth, and sixth."

It sounded as though they'd had this worked out for hours.

In a later silence, I tell Kirsten and Georgie I am never leaving the tracks again, not for the next 900 kilometers. Our perfectionist GPSs are sending us in naively straight lines, while the tracks curve safe round the bogs, mountains, and rivers. They have been etched out by people who pass through often, for centuries on horse hooves, lately on motorbike tires. It's strange to think I will only be passing through once, though I'll return enough in memory.

XVIII

A veterinarian named Pete lumbers over the urtuu mudlands. After three hours of rainy trot, his smile is our treat. He says he's surprised to find me intact—backpack, saddlebag, and pony all remembered and together. After I free the chestnut of his sweaty saddle, a man with a grin ambles him over to the horse lines for rest. In this way I move on, and so gladly does the pony. Strung to the ropes lie the next lot in wait, but the clouds are low and I feel no great draw to any of them, being tired of all the moving.

Maggie suggests I eat. I still can't tell what her exact function as steward is. In theory, she's spectating a live show of humans slowly falling to pieces.

I scarper to the dim-lit ger, where people sit variously on beds, chairs, and floor around the brown central fire, but no one sits at the rear, which is the place of honor. Kirsten's head appears on the threshold while I'm slurping soupy noodles.

"You coming, Lara?"

"I think I'm going to eat these, be rude not to finish them—you go, you go."

Whatever caused the great hurry?

Past-rider Lucy told me the food would be inedible, but I eat it all. I'm so hungry. If I'm served a sheep's testicle, I will find it delicious, like my mother with a leftover apple stalk on the moor.

I spent a fussy childhood pushing fish fingers into my pockets and fearing sauces that concealed cauliflower. This noodle soup is clear. It makes no attempt to hide the fatty meat. Later I'll read of author Uuganaa Ramsay's travels from her home in Mongolia to the United Kingdom, where she felt the pub soup tasted like dirty water and the orange juice made her twitch. She now lives in Glasgow and has written a memoir called *Mongol*, in which she reflects on bringing up her son—who has Down's syndrome— in Scotland. Until recently, the word "Mongol" was used to describe someone with Down's in English, and part of the memoir investigates the lingering prejudice Uuganaa and her son, Billy, encounter in the UK.

I gulp while the doctor drones on, stroking his beard at the lagging-behind of Georgie's twin, who apparently held second place to Devan on the first leg yesterday.

"I cannot believe Georgie Johnston is ahead of her brother. How did that happen?"

He has seen James's muscles and decided they mean victory. His voice is heavy, loud. I should be working to undermine his private-school ease, but I have noodles and a race on my brain. I play the game in my head instead, imagining him lying down—but even then he's controlled and bold, so I envisage looking into him long enough that his eyes shift away, and finally, I land on a satisfying vision of him snoozing, retired from his chattering throne. People are lovely when they let go of their faces.

When the doctor turns to ask me a question, I'm distracted by his horrid good looks. I mumble a diversionary reply. He and Maggie lean back with their eyebrows raised in laughter, and I turn away with a noodle on my lower lip, waiting for their confusion to settle. I've got no idea what I'll say next.

Shouts from the outside. Through the cinematic frame of the door, a stocky Black Beauty bucks his way through a rodeo show, twisting his body in defiance. A man is yelping in delight at the other end of the rope. This is Georgie's next horse. I give thanks for the food and scuttle out to find mine, settling on a dun, a tan horse with a black stripe down his back.

Four o'clock. Ten hours into this alarmingly long second day, we tear away from the urtuu. I tense my legs against the strain and flex of the dun's torrential gallop. Georgie's horse leads the charge, no sign of Kirsten ahead. I suppose we're less Fun Bus, more "chasing pack," now.

From a camp, two women and their boys lean their bodies back to wave and shout. We return their greetings with gooseberry eyes, holding tight to our charges. If incessant galloping was how the Mongol soldiers' days were spent, I ask myself if they just wanted all of the space and none of the kingdoms. Movement without settlement. I imagine they moved on happily and swiftly after devastating libraries in Baghdad and irrigation systems in Iran, obsessed with paths rather than places.

✦

"Where are you going?" shouts a Buddhist monk at a horse and rider in an oft-told story.

"Ask my horse," shouts the rider.

Their bolt is too fast for us to check our direction. We wait for it to run its course. At first standstill, Georgie studies the maps while I stare at the sky and feel the dun pony's breathing in my tummy. Quickly she links up to a gallop again, taking my pony with her. On this matter we're in conflict: Georgie wants to let the ponies run as long as they want, while I'd like to contain their boundlessness and preserve the energy they're expending as we shoot through merging lands.

We come to an unfinished road and ride up its side. See how it cuts through the earth. As a typical tourist, I cry inwardly at the concrete. I've heard they call it progress. Why a single road here should upset me I can't say—as though this place needs to be pristine while my city back in England is a blocked nose of concrete, trapping a whole mass of green beneath it. Ulaanbaatar too. Such unsoft stuff. I think we feel braver for it in London, bigger inside it, whatever braver and bigger might lead to.

International companies are building the infrastructure they need to mine newly discovered minerals and metals in Mongolia. As ever, capital seems to require the whole earth for its market.

From their tarmac mound, two lonely roadworkers beckon us but we gallop on, away from the day's bad weather. Georgie's map book points out a temple dedicated to the seventeenth-century Buddhist leader Zanabazar, slightly off route. We haven't the time to stop for a visit, but I do wonder. How can a temple rise up out of grass and wind and silence?

When the Mongolian People's Republic was established in 1924, purists bombarded monasteries and temples, erasing a touchstone of Buddhist culture. I can't continue beyond the word "culture" without feeling a bit ill. It's difficult to write about, so much like a jellyfish in a net—only parts sift out, and most gets destroyed in the defining of it, especially by a foreigner like me, with my knowing tones and reliance on "facts."

Many temples are merely converted gers, which probably survived in disguise. The temple to Zanabazar, though, is a building that pulled through. It was founded in the 1790s by Bogd Khan, Mongolia's first lama king, who also created the world's first national park, Bogd Khan Uul.

Blue sky, blue sky, where have you been—haunting the south with your terrible gleam. After thirty hours in hiding, the sun reveals herself and we pause at a river marsh to let our friends gulp shiny water. Georgie walks on with her pony. I hear his hooves plopping through water above sanded pebbles, and the sound of a still evening as he reaches the other side.

Up the simple ridge we go, leaning forward over the ponies' shoulders. I have named this horse Dunwoody, mainly because I have a lot of spare time in which to think up such things. It's Richard the photographer's surname, and I pronounce it Dun-*woo*-dee, as in "woohoo," though I'm not sure that's right. The habit of naming helps me regulate the journey, like a botanist who navigates nature via Latin plant appellations. Structure.

Herders here usually refer to their horses by color because there are too many to name. Besides, one horse can arrive in the world brown and depart it white, where another might evolve in one winter from dun to gray. Herders are attentive to their changing appearances. It's a nice template for imagining a being without fixing its identity, given we each travel through so many in our lives.

◆

The hill leaves Dunwoody wheezing. I let him slow in case he's having a breakdown. Georgie rides on ahead to increase her chances of making the fifth urtuu before 8:30 p.m. Meanwhile, Dunwoody indulges my sympathy, insisting on a grass feast every five strides. I'm only half engaged, occasionally shipping forth letters of persuasion to his ears. *Dear Pony, you do not know what time is. Time is being early. Let us get going? Tufts of grass, banana-skin hats, whatever else—the whole charade—please come along.* I like the grass too, like to let it amaze me.

8:15 p.m. Some 30 kilometers ahead, Devan misnavigates her route from urtuu 5 to urtuu 6, riding the long way around. In her interview with ABC before she began the race, she took pains to explain how her father, an ultramarathon runner and U.S. Marine, had been training her in navigation. "Endurance is in my blood," she finished.

Ever so slowly we inch towards the objects of distance, a mouthful of grass per three strides. By the time Dunwoody lollops me into the station, he is wearing a lipstick of green sauce. I peer forth to the corners of his mouth with a mixture of admiration and despair, like a mother leading a child home from an ice-cream-filled day.

When I dismount, he moors his mouth to the ground and refuses to move. Pete the vet has to walk over to us to take the heart rate. Thirty seconds pass hushed as he holds the stethoscope to Dunwoody's chest. Recalling the earlier hyperventilation, I think, Oh poop, we've overdone it, his rate's too high. Pete turns to face me.

"Well, forty-eight. That's the lowest post-forty-kilometer heart rate I've ever taken on the Derby."

I do not notice who takes Dunwoody from me, nor do I think to inquire after him later. I run up the hill for the loo, and bound on past it to loosen my muscles—harp-string tight. At the ridge, the view is sky, the last of a blue evening. Horses surround the station, suspending it in a dome of calm. I take in the full view and decide that this, here, is truly the valley of nothingness. I seem to think the same in every earthly bowl we reach.

Dear Ma,

Two days have passed. We've got 800 kilometers left. I'm pinned to one question: How will I make it to the end of this race with knees that have taught themselves to throb (knees mend but tights don't—Mrs. Nunes), a tummy clenched small (lunch is for wimps—I've read it somewhere), and sleep deprivation burrowing into my resolve (am certainly not dying—except very slowly like the rest of us)? I feel like a turnip that's just been yanked from the earth. It's as though this is life as they lit it, as they meant it to be before the beginning of time, but my body can't get used to it.

The sun has faded and I've retired to an eerie ger, where I've just been rolling up and down in my sleeping bag, bathing in an expanse of floor—so much room after last night's chicken farm. Those riders are scattered across the steppe this evening, spidering the map beside hearts of fur.

I am enjoying the movement from home to home, perhaps because you raised us into a cyclical life—yo-yoing between Appleshaw and London, I became fond of packing, collecting, rushing, racing, leaving things behind. Maybe it was excessive that I also liked moving between bedrooms in each place, but the beds of my absent brothers let me shake off any sodden thoughts collecting in my own room.

You see, Ma, I think I stain the spots I inhabit. When I sit in a corner to write a letter, I can't sit there again. It feels nice to avoid the memory of me—or maybe I just lust after the new.

Ideally I'd forget our address because honestly I mistrust all that it means. When the Soviets tried to introduce arable farming to the steppe in the 1920s, nomads would often plant a plot and not return for the harvest. Obviously the Soviets were disrupting their way of life, and why should they yield? But also, why tie yourself to a place?

"Perhaps my children will live in stone houses and walled towns—not I," said some khan in devotion to tented life. The refusal to rely on the same patch of land to perform year in, year out, resonates with the idea that you can't depend on one place—or one person—to keep producing the same effect. But why let their inconstancy disappoint, when you can simply move on?

I can't help thinking humans might not be the only ones who feel tied. What about buildings stuck on plots and trees planted in mud? None leads as mobile a life as a ger. The poor house in Appleshaw, fixed there in Hampshire. Though her stillness will help me to slow any galloping motion in my chest when I return, she herself might like to click her ligaments and leave England too.

I sat cross-legged in the corner of the tent, watching Kirsten rummage in her pack while I munched my last fruit bars to stave off the exhaustion. The doctor had told Kirsten that her partner back in Perth thought she was still in the city hospital recovering from fainting on briefing day. Her mood was tempestuous as a result.

Kirsten had reached the urtuu forty-five minutes before the cutoff time, but she hadn't moved on. We feared that families between stations wouldn't know about the race or expect guests. She'd only have made it a quarter of the way to the next urtuu before the trackers penalized her movement. We imagined she'd have had to sleep on cold ground, tying her pony's legs in hobbles only half effective before worrying the night away, a vision of her horse hop-hop-hopping off without her.

Despite all the tent space, the night felt hospital-like. I preferred to be either packed in or alone entirely. Around the tarred fire, crew members chatted about matters once normal to us—television shows, London riots, and then a car mechanic. The doctor held the limelight, splattering his predictable English lines about the ger, but nothing much could bother me since sleep was so near. When we English get to foreign countries, I think something happens to our sense of humor. It's as though whatever it was our wit was created for disappears. Our chins quiver, our proud noses lead us through.

Meanwhile, Richard was shuffling round the ger, shamelessly pouring out cups of Chinggis Khan vodka for riders. I accepted a cup even though it was likely to sour the pain in my muscles. Soon after, I overheard the doctor mention Richard and the Grand National in the same sentence. Oh my. Our photographer was a famous jockey. Did he win the Grand National? I asked my neighbors.

The tent tripped over itself in the shock—how could I not know? He'd ridden in Britain's biggest jump race fourteen consecutive years, won it twice in 1986 and '94, the year I was born, and been three-time Champion Jockey. I looked at Richard anew. What was he doing here, mucking in at the whims of the earth when all the Isles' racetracks awaited him?

Lying on my tummy, I pressed my pen into Winnie-the-Pooh. I like writing down snippets of a day, not just to record the past, but to get a sense of the present by retraveling time up to my seated, ceased point. The notebook was wet and overwhelmed, but here was the only place I could speak as though I would never be heard and write as though the world had no reading, only words lodged with the eyeless gods.

After two sentences I was distracted by Georgie fainting beside the fire. Tsetsgee, the chief interpreter, had planted a forest of needles in her back for the pain, but this seemed to have overwhelmed her. Medical assistance was meant to come with a three-hour penalty, but none of us said a thing as the doctor and nurse rushed to hold her wrists and forehead. I winced at the commotion, as though Georgie's vulnerability might lie within me, too.

I added a half phrase to my two sentences in Winnie-the-Pooh and nodded off. Soon they'd be illegible, sucked back into the pages during the storms headed our way.

The crew goes chit, chat, sleep.

Like most other teenagers I was not, at this time, in the habit of writing. I had written the occasional letter that veered off course (*Horse, you really ought to take up writing. I haven't had a single letter, not even a neigh*) and confided sporadically in diaries (*Dear god, my school is so petty. They told me off because I stuck a Post-it note on a teacher's back*), but there wasn't much. Not like nowadays when I rush to find a pen with the intensity of an oracle in a fit (though I'm merely a thing in situ, elbowing my way through time).

After the second day racing, there'd be little time for reflection. I wouldn't confide a single further sentence in Winnie-the-Pooh. If matters worsened, my only skill would be to let loose laughter, an expulsion of the fury I might otherwise have felt—fury at being here, at having thought it would be fun to be here.

The single written artifact from my early life is a diary I sporadically wrote between the ages of twelve and fourteen, which I recently read through. Its curiosity is its animal obsession. No one thought of me as an animal lover—too errant—yet the brief entries mention little more than pets.

22 March
Decided I wanted a parrot. Looked at parrots in a pet shop which was overpriced.

23 April
I did throw Dido's poodle in the pool, but was helping it to find courage, etc. etc.

Dateless
I'm going to breed hamsters.

It wasn't an animal-mad childhood—there was barely a dog in sight and only the occasional hamster. Yet I was gripped by books like *Shadow the Sheepdog*; *Fury, Son of the Wilds*; *The Story of Ferdinand* (the bull); and *The Cow Who Fell in the Canal*. My favorite film was *Racing Stripes*, with its talking zebra and horses;

more recently I'd enjoyed *Madagascar* and *Madagascar 2*, whose despotic King Julien, a ring-tailed lemur, I can still quote at length.

The diary drones on in purple felt-tip letters:

> 3 May
>
> I don't know if I've told you, but for the last couple of weeks I've been wanting a bunny but mummy doesn't like change, insists that bunnies aren't good pets. . . . She keeps on saying, "But what do bunnies do? They hop around and shiver." And I say, "Well what do hamsters do?" and she said, "Sit on their hind legs and look sweet and climb and play." But that's just because she had one when she was little.
>
> The next day we went to the Fish Bowl pet shop but all the rabbits had red eyes which I didn't like. Then some days later we went to the Hurlingham pet shop and they have a nice bunny, but it didn't have floppy ears so I didn't buy it, although they said they were getting new ones in next week, so I'll go back.

I never mention humans, which gives the sense that I was friendless, although I did think I had friends at the time.

The day I read this diary through, I hollered to my brother, Harold, next door. "Why d'you think I was so keen on animals, when you never were?"

"Er, I dunno, because you relate to them?"

There was a pause between our bedrooms. This was my curly-haired younger brother, the one who used to perform with his vacuum cleaner for the crowds outside my school, back in the years when I was shy. I had witnessed his shows, peeping out from Mum's green coat.

He picks up the pause. "Because you want to be an animal."

14 May
Went to Pets at Home. Here's my long list in order of all my pet ideas in the past weeks: monkey, penguin, hamster breeding, parrot, piglet, donkey, giraffe, zebra, rabbit, house rabbit. And after an hour at Pets at Home, I finally came to a decision. A dog. A golden cocker spaniel, or black.

I never did get a dog, but in the years when the wrath of teachers washed weekly through my system, horses and hamsters were my anti-authoritarian medicine. I'd even subconsciously adopted some of their behaviors. I snorted to clear my throat, ate from the ground, licked my plate, and massaged my back on lampposts in the same manner a horse will dig her bottom into a fence. For breakfast I liked SUCCEED Digestive Conditioning, an oily oat paste that came in syringe form (*"Insert into your horse's mouth"*), of which Aunt Lucinda kept me in high supply.

I tell myself that if I had my way, I'd be living in an unassembled valley, just a stream, me, and the green. But I can't decide if I will like it in practice. I keep trying it out halfheartedly, which makes for impure results. Things suck me back into the network—my stomach wails, for instance, and I trudge out of the idyll to a Tesco supermarket. Where else can a wild huntress find her food in February?

The Christmas after the race, my father gave me a picture of a galloping leopard. He said it reminded him of me. Yet he was the one who didn't want me spending too much time with horses, for the horse neither answers back nor pays the bills. Then again, animals were our first teachers. Thousands of years ago, our dances, languages, and rituals passed from their behavior into ours. The frogs taught us jumping and the plants taught us patience and who taught me to flee? To feel tentatively confident and always free?

We humans seem to have put a lot of energy into separating ourselves from nature. In films we create fantasy characters who can talk to animals even though we all used to know how to do so, and the animals have been talking to us all along. I think we forget that they see us back. To the zoos we shuffle in search of their kingdoms, but we find them there suppressed in cages. They barely look at us; they're barely animals. The race reclaims me as an animal—my original form, my rawest self, my favorite way to be.

XIX

I rise on day 3 to find my legs are lead. Outside, a weak sunlight washes the valley. Breakfast does not appear. It's not a meal they eat here, says Richard in his morning face, hair a little startled by the gravity change. Only *airag* at this hour, he continues, and I continue in my mind, Airag at six in the morning? I'd rather no breakfast.

Airag is fermented horse milk. It's the national drink. The herder in charge of start camp said some men drink up to twenty liters a day in the summer. Apparently it's very healthy, a sort of cleansing agent. It has a sour taste.

Richard pops up on the lighter side of the ger to photograph me brushing my teeth. Is this worthy material? Maybe the sawing action of my arm on my teeth reflects some inner struggle. Small things seem to give Richard energy. I've seen him photographing blades of grass just as intently as he does the humans upon them.

Later today, I'll find out that a neck injury forced Richard to retire from professional jockeying, after which he trekked to the North and South Poles, struggling to settle after a life of leaping. Lately he has found photography, and travels to capture horse sport in all its incarnations—in the UK, Ireland, Sudan, Afghanistan, and here in Mongolia. Last night he revealed he had once swapped sports with Aunt Lucinda for a charitable cause—she jockeying, he eventing. "Your aunt ended up with a bloody nose," he chuckled, seeming so calm now, in his late forties.

I'm anxious to ride out of the urtuu at exactly 0700 hours, sounding just like that, in the official oh-seven-hundred voice. Kirsten and Georgie are drifting about under their backpacks, the latter gradual, the former scuttling, neither seeming ready. I hear each of them asking about breakfast like I did.

I click the satellite tracker to "on" and walk down the horse line, tuning into the ponies' eyes. Then I notice Richard's camera stalking my concentration face, and erupt with laughter.

Each time I visit a pony's head I feel as though I'm waking him from winter hibernation. The first pony falls back to sleep after browsing me. Richard says I should take the bare-ribbed chestnut at the end of the line, but when we walk up to him we find he has a bleeding mouth. I can't pull at a mouth like that, have it hurting and staining the grass red. We hold hands with a horse through its mouth, as we tinker the bit this way and that. When Aunt Lucinda was eight she had a pony who refused to move if she so much as touched his mouth through the reins. His tactic taught her to soften her hands.

After her *Bloody hell, no* response on pony-picking advice, she sent a follow-up email. "Heaven knows what you look for—but small and tough with a never-say-die look in its eye."

Since neither Georgie nor Kirsten has appeared, I ask the tall man of the Enkhtaivan family if he can suggest another wild one. "Khurdan?" I say, since "fast" is the closest word to "wild" I know in Mongolian. The man seems to want a good horse for me. He plucks out a platinum-blond—almost dog-sized—and lets it scamper a circle on the rope.

Two boys are drafted in to help saddle up the pony. They lean their arms on his shoulders while he kicks limbs in all directions. Clearly he's a catapult, and I don't want to be the first thing he slings. Might someone like to get on before me? A man who has been leaning against his white truck volunteers and swings a leg aboard. The catapult—who I'll soon name Barbie for his blond mane—spirals and bucks with his left eye flickering white, tail flying like a snake. Just before he might be thrown, the man jumps to the ground.

With Kirsten and Georgie mounted, I must get on. I place my foot in the stirrup and leap, knowing the lengthened endurance stirrups won't anchor me to his buck. He swerves and propels his head into the herder, who rams into him, demanding control.

We go sideways up the hill. The creature's back is tense, the creature's back will fling. My focus is split between the body beneath me and the majestic steps of the tall man leading us, his burgundy cloak currying the ground. He hands me the rope at the ridge. Before my smile is complete, the cow-colored pony charges me into the morning. *And upward, ever upward, the wild horses held their way.*

0713. Departed. I'm hyperaware of the minutes lost waiting for Kirsten and Georgie. All those times I left tapping feet waiting, all

those afternoons we rigged the wooden classrooms into disorder—
they make no sense in comparison, because why wait until now to
get on with things?

Well, what use are questions to the past?

Three hours ahead were the riders in second and third. I was so
surprised to be roughly fifth, having been last for the first leg of
the race, that my focus was not on catching up with those ahead as
much as it was on keeping in front of the riders behind me. I was
worried I'd fall back again.

My mother worries a lot too. But she loves it. She lives in a
worry. It colors her dreams. Her whole existence is worrisome,
partly I think because when her worries come true she feels a sense
of victory, and when they don't, she feels her worrying has paid off
because it has ordered the future into compliance.

Barbie was small. My torso was long enough to tip us off
course. When I look at the photo now, I suppress my urge to ring
the RSPCA. The head structure and bone size of Mongolian
ponies classify them, in genetic terms, as horses. Besides, size isn't
presumed to determine performance in Mongolia. Wrestlers are
never categorized by weight, and smaller ponies aren't necessarily
slower or weaker. This tiny creature was the strongest I'd ridden
so far.

As we edged along a flood plain—lumps of rock hanging off the
slopes rising at our sides—small talk occasionally reared its ugly
head. Sometimes we chattered to the ponies. Mostly we dribbled
through silence. I'd no idea what any of us was thinking. Kirsten
pointed out the little mice in the ground, which looked like the

hamsters I once doted on. Now they were hazard-digging enemies along with the marmots.

As the hours passed, the hamsters seemed the only real things. They sat grooming themselves above the ground before whipping down holes when our hooves neared. Who knows what happened when they accidentally descended the hole of a cousin they disliked. There must have been thousands of hamster squabbles going on in the earth.

Our race was strung-out and placid in comparison. The only thing we had to hole-punch the drawl of the leg was an ovoo. We circled it thrice and walked on against the sun. All morning she beat us along and laid us bare.

When Georgie dropped behind and shrank into a dot, Kirsten and I looked at each other, not speaking the words. There was no wood to touch in the race; I hadn't seen a tree since the city. So we waited. To avoid existential combustion, I focused on the yaks grazing their way up the riverbed. Maybe they were full of advice I was unable to access. I turned my head away from them, then back again, shedding laughter for the need to release something into the air.

It was some time before the dot in the distance enlarged into Georgie. She said she had a stomach bug, I caught her on camera describing it. Assured she was fine, we left her behind again, not wanting her slow pony to congeal our progress. I began flinging questions at Kirsten as we hurried away.

"Have you ever done endurance riding before, back in Perth?"

"Me? Yeah, I done tons of the stuff."

Until now I've let the ponies canter or trot as they like. Kirsten says that in endurance, horses canter in rhythm for lengthy periods to level their heart rates. Is this how Devan has disappeared so far into the lead? I don't know why the other endurance riders aren't keeping up with her.

Kirsten is teaching me. We're supposedly competing in this moment, but it's hopeless to jostle in the pale of 1,000 kilometers. The kind of solemn seriousness you would aim for in a marathon runner is made a fool of by the fourteen-hour days.

Later in the leg, a yellow rapeseed field erupts from the steppe's muted color palette. It's a travel writer's habit to compare her surroundings to where she has come from, and I can only think of the agricultural fields of England, those ones we sail by in our cars, combed and contained, broad and immovable. Things look so different through windows. Fields appear cake-like. Warm, perfect.

As we drift up the side of this plot, Richard's jeep rumbles into sight. I light up at the thought of him. He'll be wearing that wry expression, the look of knowing what's beyond us.

"Have you fallen off yet?" he asked me last night for the second time.

"Oh, you will," he muttered with a knowing look. "Everyone does."

I nearly walked out the tent.

I'm not scared of the falls. I worry more about slow, subtle destruction: my stirrup leathers blistering my calves, for instance. Or my mind losing its way.

Kirsten is talking about some kind of shortcut, but I refuse to leave the tracks. We split up. Blond-maned Barbie and I go it alone on the sandy footing. His name has stuck for two hours now, not too bad. Just as I'm loosening into Barbie's scrappy canter, he stumbles on a hidden marmot hole. His legs buckle, he somersaults, and over his head I ping. The day slams to a halt.

I crouch and watch him try to stand. His foreleg is trapped in the girth strap. He cannot run away. "Horses do not return like dogs," I whisper in the voice of David Attenborough. No whistling, no finger-clicking.

When I step towards him, he hops away like the kitchen mouse who used to ignite our late nights in London. There's a strangeness, for a horse, to losing a rider—the centaur vanishes, his partner becomes a predator at his side. He can feel unsettlingly light and flighty. The strap around Barbie's leg looks as though it's about to break, which will let him bolt over the boglands while I hum my way after him.

I prowl shyly with my eyes on the ground. I don't want him thinking he's my target. Each second feels the size of the steppe.

Leap. I catch his reins. Breath pours out of me. He fidgets as I untangle him, peeling back the whites of his eyes. "Stand still, woah." Every time I try to mount, he pirouettes away. At the urtuus, herders have held the horses for me. Alone, over and over again, I prove useless. Scrapping safety, I lean inwards and climb as he shunts into canter. Covered in dust, we're one again.

Other than some pain in my thumb, I am fine, and so seems Barbie. Without a god to thank, I lose myself wondering where the luck came from.

Richard reappears just as we're sprinting away from the accident. I shoot wary glances for hamster cities ahead while I scream to him how we fell, jotting the drama into the passing air with one hand.

I'm not sure if he replies. All I can see is his camera-nose peeking out of the jeep's sunroof, striking from afar. He must feel victorious. Eleven a.m. and already his prophecy from last night fulfilled.

Honestly, I think I loved the fall—I'd had enough of meandering. Quick shock, full time, very real. Splat.

XX

At the sixth urtuu, Kirsten circles on foot like a seagull plotting at the harbor. I promise a quick changeover and she says she'll wait. None of us wants to ride alone. We've imagined a thousand possibilities by now, not least falling horses and time-worn loneliness. I skip the meal. The interpreter at the station holds her long glossy hair above her shoulders. Her jeans and ironed jacket make me think she has come from the city. Spending days on the steppe may be almost as new to her as it is to me. "I don't know how horses work," a city person I met in Ulaanbaatar told me.

"Lara, I am so pleased you are in fifth."

I hitch my face in a grin. The ranking, the compliment unexpected, and the idea of what she might say next.

"You are one of the three girls I want to win!"

I'm keen to know who the other two girls are, and this desire to know leaves me unsure of myself. Am I involved in something deeply serious, or am I just a piece in a board game?

Maybe such thinking is a symptom of my tiredness, or of my outlook as a surface-skating youth who hasn't yet decided how much to invest in the world. In endless tweets, bored race organizers in Ulaanbaatar contemplate whether anyone will catch Devan Horn. "What an absolute Viking she is," one of them says. They note she takes half the time of other riders to change horses.

None of us is much in comparison to the Mongol Empire's postal system. Thanks to the horses, messages strapped to riders' backs could travel 450 kilometers in twenty-four hours. Yesterday my total was a measly 120, Devan's 140. Then again, it did take 60,000 empire soldiers an entire year to advance 1,000 kilometers against opposing forces, and this, at the time, was apparently seen as record speed.

Alone we're faster than an army, yet we make progress only in the name of sport. I've heard it said that sport is war in disguise, but hopefully sporting events have meaning beyond victory versus loss. How else was the Netherlands football team so internationally loved in the 1960s despite blowing the matches that mattered? The winning moments dominate the news, but people who make up sports teams and armies must live lives of continual flux—95 percent ordinariness, 5 percent brilliance.

Maybe I saw a preview of life in this world before I got here and, as the brilliant parts rushed before me, thought, *Yeah, I'll go to that place*, and signed on, not thinking of the in-between parts.

Kirsten helps me choose my next pony.

"Not that one—he's got bad feet."

I'd never have noticed.

In a beige lunchtime light, we pootle off the hill of the sixth urtuu. Over the spread of hills behind us is a former capital of the Mongol

Empire, Kharkhorum, once filled with monasteries, mosques, and churches, all flattened now.

The Mongols were dreaded in Europe and dreaded in Japan, yet their so-called barbaric empire tolerated all religions, and still today Ulaanbaatar is home to temples, Baha'i places of worship, churches, and mosques. Chinggis Khan himself was religiously open (according to the chroniclers), in the hope that at least one of the gods would show appreciation for his life's work.

I understand his armies could be devastating (and those of his descendants—his grandson Kubilai Khan conquered China, while another grandson, Batu Khan, took Baghdad), but perhaps it's refreshing that he had no pretentious crusader ambitions for his conquests, no attempt to assert the force of some god. His desire for power was more honest. More like Devan's.

Some of the Derby legs fade in my memory. The leg to urtuu 7 felt distant, impossibly far from home. We roved through a hilly side country I found underwhelming. The pony below me, who I noted later as 7: *the slow-canterin' chestnut*, seesawed on one leg while my right knee loosened, and Kirsten's pony acted as though he'd never been ridden, offering, in the spirit of an insect, a series of jumps sideways.

We dodge herds of nibbling goats whose heads are tuned into some conference inside the earth. I sense their disdain for our motion, the way we pass them fast and carry on just as fast. Oh but who am I to feel the judgment of a goatherd? I try talking to Kirsten, expect some revelations, and receive none. Maybe it's just an English thing, wanting to harvest background. Neither Kirsten nor Devan has been interested in me. I'm not sure I'd have much to say for myself if they were, but the conversation feels imbalanced when I'm asking all the questions.

Maybe I'm disappointed because the rocking backs of horses sustain a rhythm suited to long and searching conversations. On the rare evenings she was home and I was in Appleshaw, Aunt Lucinda and I sometimes rode together. She would let her reins drop and begin conducting her hands to accompany her words, which she spoke at twice the beat of her horse's walk. Often she tried to diagnose the world, or diagnose me, forcing cold moments of questioning.

If I ever gathered the courage to question her back, she tended to deflect, as though rebounding from acute pain. Whether this was to compensate for years of nationwide attention or simply a result of her war-era parents persuading her never to talk about herself, I can't tell—she remains emotionally undeclared. Alcohol is a rare subject on which she'll reveal herself. She hates to drink, says "I can't bear the feeling of being out of control."

As for Kirsten and me, we manage one exchange in the hour.

"So, question: How many hamsters do you reckon there are in Mongolia, Kirsten?"

"Oh, crikey. A billion?"

"No! Really, five hundred million."

The discussion rumbles and fizzles out into the scuttling hooves beneath us.

Later we show the horses to a stagnant water hole. Flies buzz, hardly flying, as though they have come for a party and found its atmosphere unexpectedly grave. I take the pony through at a trot to splash his coat. Kirsten follows suit.

At a certain dip in the hour, Georgie's snorting horse gallops in and tanks her up the hill ahead.

"Hallo!"

Additional words fall back, unable to form at such speed. Kirsten and I push for a canter to keep up but our ponies can't match Georgie's pony. Kirsten curses hers as he moves sideways, all the way up the hill. Meanwhile, my thumb and knee are wailing their way through an opera. My brain reminds itself that pain is created and all we must do is puff it out. Be a good chimney.

When we descend a sandy track on a plain streaked with grass, I feel we might be nearing the station, though Kirsten says we're miles off. The clouds have arranged themselves in dancerly fashion, like Arabic script, and the sky looks as if it could be a map of the world. Beyond us a figure is striding out of his ger towards a singular horse. From this far away there's room to remember that the land he marches neither begins nor ends. He doesn't own a specific bit of it.

There's no land ownership on the steppe, since the earth isn't for sale; by contrast, every patch of England seems to be buyable, even some waterways. Ibn Khaldun, historian of the fourteenth century, felt nomads were "removed from all the evil habits that infected the hearts of settlers." He might've deemed the right to buy property one such evil.

Farther into the basin, I rub my sweaty eyelids at a sight across the way: three horses and riders, peeling the hill in their coming, striding to the tempo of the sky-high afternoon. They turn out to be Georgie, Clare (another British rider), and Kiwi Chloe. They have entered from the wrong direction. They must've been lost in the hills. How else have we caught up astride our sideways clowns? Three cheers to Kirsten for navigating.

Only Devan's ahead of us now. Clare and Chloe say they haven't glimpsed her since the start line two days ago. She hovers as a faceless snowman in my mind, sinister, stuck. Stuck in the lead.

The smell of animal dung hangs in the air at the seventh urtuu. Sun plats the surrounding hills; the brightness is striking. Charles, the steward in his early thirties, rules the roost, while Richard stands on a spot of stale earth, swatting the heat, his camera apparently exiled to his jeep. I pull the pony into trot, fearing he'll look lame on the hard ground, but the vet decides he looks fine. I slump to a relieved halt to wait for his heart rate to drop. Sweat drips from my helmet onto the tip of my nose.

"If you want his heart rate to drop, walk him up and down into the wind," says Charles, rocking from foot to foot.

The authority in his tone surprises me, and I'm unsure why he's helping. Only now can I place his accent as South African. Kirsten says Afrikaans is his first language and he doesn't really like speaking English. Apparently he won the race in its first year, alongside Shiravsamboo Galbadrakh, the only Mongolian who entered. Addicted to the steppe and the strangeness of the race, Charles returns annually to steward.

I ask him if I can borrow some toilet paper, but my appeal is met with a glare. I traipse on with the pony, looking down at my thumb. It's red and warm after the fall from Barbie. Laughing bones. I seem to have so many.

Something about the middle of the race—its heat and how unshapely it is—creates in me an apathy as we judge the next horses. Tiny but brilliant, Barbie denied nature's conformation rules. I can no longer use a horse's appearance to forecast how it will go. Two men from the Damdinbazar family allot me the "best horse at the station," who we're saddling together when Undrakh, an interpreter with a city-style Mohawk, sidles up to me and hands over a roll of loo paper. "Please return it," he mumbles. I see Charles looking over at me (Oh! the romantic tension), and extend my stride to the toilet.

I haven't mentioned that I need the paper to stop my blue jodhpurs from going purple, but as of this morning I've been bleeding onto the saddle. I forgot to take any of the pills that keep my period away. Its arrival strikes me as odd, perhaps because I feel the Derby has suspended ordinary life's cycles. If it's true that periods rarely arrive in times of uncertainty, then this might mean I've relaxed into the race. Surrendered myself to its form.

I'm two steps from mounting when Charles makes another announcement to us.

"You can make it to urtuu nine today."

I look down at the time, alarmed. Two urtuus in six hours? The legs have been taking four hours each. We can't expect to reach urtuu 9 until tomorrow morning. Devan trots through my mind with her head held high. So goes the Mongol Derby press release: *The way she's riding at the moment she'll be very difficult to pass, but you just never know.*

Charles walks forward to my next horse's shoulder. He places his hand on the mane and looks up at me with furrowed brows. "You're on the best horse here."

I can't get my head around this outburst of belief from the aloof steward. If only I were in a historical flurry with some scroll to be delivered to the Caspian Sea by midnight, this would no longer be silly, no longer be sport.

✦

The Khangai Mountains are coming, says the map book, which alternately presents helpful and useless information. *Keep an eye out for the very beautiful woman living at urtuu 11*, it says, a few pages ahead.

Tsendiin Damdinsüren, a twentieth-century Mongolian poet, wrote about these mountains in winter.

> Girded in a mantle of white,
> Glistening in a cap of snow,
> The Khangai range is bridled
> By a blue ribbon of ice-cold rivers.

I can see their surfaces dry in the distance, while towards my right ear Kirsten and Clare are hurrying out of camp in the wrong direction. I shout them back and they relaunch ahead of me. When I catch up with Clare, she is bent to the ground beneath her jittering pony.

"Dropped my GPS! Thought I might as well pee whilst I was off."

Clare is about to get married. Being from the same country, we interact as though we're already acquainted. Her gear is emblazoned with sponsors' names, from horse-feeding companies to an insurance broker.

"I'll be really trying to win," she told an equestrian magazine before the race.

In the pause while I wait for her to finish peeing, I glimpse my own condition—a string of petty aches from my bunions upwards.

Kirsten and Clare canter up the hard, steep mud towards the crinkled ridge. Their ponies' hooves make hammering sounds.

"Shouldn't we walk up here?" I ask behind them.

No reply.

"Do you think we should walk up here?"

Still nothing. I slow Best Horse to a walk and watch them haul up and out of my vision.

XXI

Left alone on the eighth leg of the race, I'm giddy at the thought of navigation. I pull over the brow into a sphere of rolling mountains and frown at the terrain for the energy it's about to suck from my pony. I've no longer any words for the land, though the view ahead is one my parents might classify as "beautiful," "glorious," or "quite spectacular," as if the landscape were an ornament created for human commentary.

Half an hour after being left behind, the pony and I follow two distant dots that appear and quickly disappear on the horizon. I assume them to be Clare and Kirsten, though to be honest there's no way of telling they aren't two married goats on an afternoon honeymoon. When the dots lead us too far to the left, the GPS, in a rare moment of devotion, corrects us before damage to the route is done.

Leaning off the sides of hills, we pull forward, feeling very alone, as if we're the last drops at the bottom of a wine glass. On the one hand, the pony's laissez-faire attitude makes for soothing company; on the other hand, we're barely halfway to the next station. When he's had enough of trotting, I call him a banana and tell him he'll make me cry. We're the last of the chasers, can't he see? He pricks his ears. *Urr biyiig zovoono, uul moriig zovoono.* A proverb from western Mongolia. Anger wears down the body, as a mountain wears down a horse.

On we graft through valleys of sadness, into a sedate evening sky. Twice we walk high in the center of a goat herd. Their eyes stare through us. I try not to care that we've fallen behind, yet I care ever more. I decide I was never meant to last long with the leading riders, but when we come out of the mountains onto a track, I push the pony, whom I've taken to calling Best Horse. *You must keep cantering.* That was Kirsten's advice.

He doesn't seem tired, only exceptionally grumpy. Me, I'm the same—what failed hope, what undone legs. Not long ago I was high on the excitement of the urtuu, now I'm just a frustrated cabbage, earnestly upset. This pendulum of emotions must be the joke of the human, but never before have I felt it so condensed, and rarely so convincing.

How the last kilometers stretch out so far, I do not understand. I let my head rest carelessly on my shoulders while Best Horse's ears go on ahead of me like two creatures twitching with laughter. Our slow evensong pace is un-racey. Aren't you lucky you don't have to go the whole thousand kilometers? I ask him, not wondering how he might feel to have been coopted into my ego. I get the ABC recorder out to continue my monologue. I feel this camera and I are friends, though that may just be because I've turned it into a receptacle for all my emotional debris.

A large herd of sheep canters into a cluster away from us. "I believe I might get there quicker on board one of them," I say, before closing the camera flip screen. Why are people always insulting sheep? London used to belong to sheep and shorter things. What does it mean to be sheepish, really? This horse I'm riding is sheepish. Wants his herd back.

It's funny to think of London out here. Suppose it's all I have to fall back on. I have this idea that it's my friends whose compasses center on London, but the city seems to have become a part of me too, accumulating affection for herself in the manner of an old wart. All my journeys within her skyline—I didn't like them but they happened to me, in the way fields happen to horses, and I feel no need to resent them anymore.

The Mongols who made the empire were supposedly a people without even a fixed town to their name. They didn't need to stamp the land with grand buildings. Anne Carson writes: "Towns are the illusion that things hang together somehow." Even Aunt Lucinda's sport, eventing, happens in purpose-built environments— parklands designed by historic landscapists like Capability Brown, then molded again into courses for horses. This race dangles well away from that realm. Nothing has been shaped, little mapped— the valleys are splayed out, and we are undefined.

Six o'clock. Best Horse and I wiggle our way up a weedy hillock into urtuu 8. No hope for urtuu 9 before 8:30 p.m. Maybe the others will make it.

Yet I spit shock. They are here. Kirsten, Chloe, and Clare flow around the gers, seasoned postal riders that they are.

The convergence of Cs and Ks is confusing even to me. Chloe is the Kiwi who taught me a rabbit song at start camp. Her face has been made gaunt by the race, or maybe it was already so. She's older than I am but younger than the other two. Clare is the British one with sponsors and a pink bobble on her helmet. And Kirsten's Kirsten.

I presume their ponies bolted for too long at the start of the leg, which allowed Best Horse, who never bothered exerting himself in the first place, to catch up. I glare at his bottom as a boy leads him away. How slow he made the afternoon. My face is frozen into a scowl, colored orange by the late sun, when I notice Richard trying to take a photograph. He tends to catch me grinning, as though the race is a never-ending pleasure. Around now I start forgetting to smile.

Baska the vet is quiet. He seems to let the sun go easily. Beside him I feel daft about my little tantrums on Best Horse. I'd like some of his underlying contentment. Where is my silent laugh? My droning "It's fine"?

"It's fine" comes from Mum. It's one of her main phrases. She utters it often to her children with her voice lowered. I think of it as the warrior in her, running parallel to her worries.

Urtuu 8 is a springboard into the next leg. It leans down the hill, horses ever lower on the line.

"I would love your fastest, wildest pony. The one that will gallop all the way, that will buck and bolt. The one with most life."

The interpreter translates in fewer words. I don't even look at the line of ponies. I've a new faith. Oh, *won't* the herder sympathize with the distress in my eye and the passion in my voice? The sun is setting. I am in the mood either to begin a mission or to end one.

Two tall men saunter into the bunch of sleeping ponies and draw out a chestnut. I'm careful not to share my skeptical feelings. I see a shirtless man stride past me with his tummy wobbling. His mustache is perfect. His shoulders are sunburnt. I think he will mount before I do.

In a relaxed haze, he pulls himself onto the unsaddled horse. His friends have turned to watch. Without stirrups he won't be able to grip if the pony bucks. The invention of the stirrup was pivotal for war riding. Soldiers could suspend their feet on platforms on either side of the horse's barrel, leaving their bodies free to swivel with the lance. This made them less likely to topple off while fighting.

The pony trots the topless man in large circles. People have closed into a crescent formation around him—many hands on hips. I watch the rider's tummy shaking in belated rhythm to the trot, then I peep at Richard to my left, scanning him for signs of approval. The animal is fluid in motion, but I'm upset he hasn't yet bucked.

After all their efforts in choosing, I can't be fussy. One man is nodding before me, another is tacking him up. I sprint up the incline to fill my water, and find Chloe marching back to the lines, her hair hanging heavy. She shouts that she'll wait for me if I don't stop to eat, so I take only water. It streams from a can at the hands of a crouching lady, whose eyes I feel following my form as I run back to the horse lines.

Before I'm fully on, we're off, off across the grass, away, away from home where my family must be stuffed in for sofa-breakfast, arguments flying like feathers. With every galloping horse I get farther away. There's no denying I believe I'm coming closer to something, too. I don't think it's the finish line, though that's somewhere on the list. Nor does it seem to be Devan, who is, of course, still in the lead.

Temul. It's the Mongolian word for the look in the eye of a horse charging down its own undrawn route. Nothing slows him, this new horse I'm riding, not even a pit of rocks. There must be a clot of oats in his brain. I'm temul as much as he—no idea where we're meant to be going. I fix my knees and pull him up. We wait for the others to catch us. Kirsten shuffles in aboard a horse full of sweat and asks him for canter. "Choo choo choo choo." My pony overhears. Again we are pounding.

His determination to hurl on through air is without reason. This I love. His ambivalence towards the marmot holes, I like less. But it lets me forget the competition. Makes me remember I'm here for the motion, the thrill, not the thought. His speed quells my desire to sleep.

When Secretariat won the 1973 Belmont Stakes by thirty-one lengths, he reignited the question of why horses race. What made him push himself faster after overtaking his rival, Sham, early in the race? Horses often strive to get ahead of their field, but it seemed Secretariat kept speeding up just to see what he could do. Why do we push ourselves? Perhaps not for competition, but for our causeless passions. A friend of mine says she just wants to hit a good badminton shot to "break through" herself.

The chestnut pony gallivants us into a chapter of grass, lush and smooth, boasting its basic facts: greenness, the willingness to wilt in the wind and rise again soon after. Resilience in each streak. I want to pat it all. Green is an unlucky color, according to my mother's imaginary handbook. Elsewhere it has come to symbolize all manner of goodness: resurrection, immortality, healing, and liberty—the breaking of bonds with the earth: flight. *Lo, I have created the horse*, says God in one translation of a Bedouin text. *I have molded it from the wind, I have tied good fortune to its mane. It will fly without wings. It will be the noblest of animals.*

Kirsten and I rode hard into the stormy evening. Urtuu 9 was still out of reach but we were 10 kilometers closer than we'd expected. At the ridge, my eyes leapt into an opening in the land below. A lake. A landing strip for my senses—water stretching thousands of meters into the dusking west. I was making plans for a swim when we heard a cry from the top of the hill.

"Waaittt!"

I swung round. My horse balanced on the chalky slope. Then the voice again.

"Will you waaaaaiiiiiiiiitt!"

Who would scream in this fashion? The race had been dramatic in a slow-cooking-pot way, but never so episodic or loud.

It was Chloe, on the peak. Atop her donkey. Kirsten and I carried on down.

"Wait, you fuckers!"

That is what I thought she said, though I preferred not to believe it. "You mustn't swear, it isn't ladylike," my father tells me often. "Fuck off," I reply, although half of me thinks swearing does cut the air. Kirsten and I sat still, caught between the values of the race and our reluctance to turn back up the steep hill. Urtuu 9 was within 3 kilometers and someone needed to catch Devan, or at least fulfill Charles's prophecy.

Clare, fifty meters above us, turned for Chloe while we tiptoed on down. The horses hardened themselves up to a gallop by the water. The earth was worn and their hooves echoed. I glanced at the shore and batted away my urge to eat lake. Be lake. Be beneath lake. Lungfuls of air howled through us. Mongolian myth has it that the wind comes from an old woman in heaven. In her chin she has a sack of skin containing wind, which she opens when she's angry.

Three minutes until cutoff and we were still 2 kilometers from the gers of the family at the next station. We would not make it. Now to find a place to stay.

People living in gers between urtuus didn't tend to know about the race. I was unsure what they would make of our apparition. When bicycling in England, I always want to knock on doors mainly to see if the brick houses will undo their austere façades. Canvas gers share no such affront, and from afar we could spy people outside a lakeside camp.

I wasn't able to see clearly the woman we were talking to, but by the time a man and two boys joined us, I felt a part of the network. It was as though I were in the corner shop near high school, with its memories of lollipops, cigarettes, and concrete, all standard and close to home.

Long after the family had offered us a place to stay, Kirsten was handing the phrase book to them and snatching it back in a form of linguistic hot potato. While she searched for polite things to say, such as "Thank you for your hospitality," an elder man led the ponies to a pole and tied them without leeway to stretch for grass or water. I was anxious to walk them after their final gallop or their legs would go rigid in the cold. Steam rose from their backs into thin evening air.

"Oh fuck it. Lara!" said Kirsten. "There's no word for 'hospitality' in the frickin' phrasebook."

I told her, a decade my senior, that we should see to the horses, forget the thanks.

"Wait, Lara—I've got to tell them I'm a vegetarian."

I stand by while she tries to explain this.

We tuck back into night, leading the ponies towards the lake. Two boys follow at a particular distance, which has me wondering about their intentions. They wear tight T-shirts, little signs of Ulaanbaatar sprouting on the steppe. The older men back at the gers are cloaked in heavy *dels*, which were once everyday wear for both men and women.

The pebbly shore is empty but for a brightly clad group strewn about a campfire. The ponies snort at the lake, suspicious. Perhaps they have never met so much water before. They refuse to drink. I want to strip down and swim, but with the boys at our shoulders this can't be the time—and I'm bound to the pony.

Thunder tips about in the night sky as we walk back up to camp. Kirsten leads her horse in one hand and holds two phrase books in the other. One is mine, an heirloom from Paddy, and I feel a strange guilt seeing it out and about, not knowing where he might be. The taller boy in the cap takes it now and flicks it through, stumbling over the English. Kirsten studies hers as she strides, mumbling Mongolian. Neither listens to the other. Behind us the horses are minding their business at the ends of the reins.

"Stupid!" the boy exclaims after some quiet, pointing at the book.

In a fit of enthusiasm for this word and our shared opinion regarding the shitty translations, I snatch the book from him.

"Yes, stupid!"

I throw it onto the ground.

✦

Back at camp, my eye lands on the pony's as I tie him up. His is a sweet and playful eye, running away and returning six times a second. Horses aren't so blithely passionate as lovers—they rarely look at you directly. They share love with gentle tilted heads, their eyes pulled inward. If you scratch them where they're itchy, they may niggle you back with their noses, during which I feel like an honorary horse. This pony, though sleepy, still bends away when I lift my hand to his withers. I'm sure he's got hugs stored deep inside him. Perhaps his wildness will die down overnight?

The sport of eventing operates at the threshold between tameness and wildness. The horse submits for the dance of dressage but retains her spirit to dash across country. Riders train most days and make friends with their horses. They may even dream of inviting them into their kitchens, if only the creatures would more easily fit through doors.

There are too many horses to befriend out here. Badma, who I met at the phone shop in the city, said that in spring her cousin's family sometimes takes cold foals into the ger, where they wrap them in skins and place them next to the fire. But thereafter, many of the horses live un-tame.

Kirsten and I move into an empty ger with two beds. She christens hers by flopping back onto it. We've not had beds since Ulaanbaatar. I pop outside to find the storm rolling near and a little boy who wants to play. His beaming cheeks cajole me into it. He runs, rolls, and expects me to chase but my steps are ill fitted to his scuttles and we're both clumsy with our bodies. Aunt Lucinda says I still haven't grown into mine. Then again, she says a lot of things. Says my voice hobbles along. Says I'm scatterbrained. Says I'm too relaxed.

I withdraw for exhaustion. He isn't the first strong child I've met in the last few days. An I-don't-have-a-bedtime sort of child. All those young jockeys who galloped 10 kilometers bareback for the start camp race were totally unfazed. And when I hung the herder's son upside down for hitting a fellow rider with his Coke bottle, he simply resumed his antics, victorious at the attention.

On my way back to the ger, I see a woman milking a cow. I reckon she is doing this especially for us so I tell Kirsten what she's up to—yesterday I tried the milk tea I suspect is coming our way and didn't like it. It's sweet and salty. Kirsten is crinkling plastic in search of her flashlight when the door swings open. We turn, both of us half dressed.

"Supper?" the boy pronounces slowly from the phrase book, his light shining at us.

Kirsten stands up with her headlamp mounted, which brings the boy's blue tracksuit into fluorescence. She advances in her underwear to say, "Vegetarian. Wants dinner without mutton."

Steam from cups of milky tea rises from his hands. We smile, and when he goes, leaving the tea with us, I peel my jodhpurs off.

"Jesus, Lara, what's going on with those ankles?"

Kirsten's light has landed on my feet. Ah, the site of the throbbing. Funny how patches of pain conceal themselves like the rhythm inside a song. My brain is too fatigued to attend to the various aches. I feel like one of those historic ruins, unbothered by the state of myself. I poke the spongy swelling in my ankle and fish into my bag of pills, hoping for ibuprofen. In a fit of boredom at start camp, I de-packaged six types of pills and put them into one bag. I can't tell what is antibiotics, ibuprofen, paracetamol, water purifier, Pepto-Bismol, or vitamin C. I take three pills and pray.

"Where's the tea gone?" I ask Kirsten.

She sniggers from her sleeping bag. "Tipped the fuckers onto the dirt at the edge of the bloody ger, didn't I."

I've heard that some families toss milk into the air to invoke the protection of spirits at the start of a journey, and people sometimes place a bowl of cream outside their gers to honor the earth, land, and sky—baigal. But on page 22 of our map book, it says, *Don't spill any milk, it's very unlucky.*

Dinner never comes. Vegetarianism is untranslatable this evening. I eat a handful of Kirsten's walnuts and lie down listening to the storm. My tummy rumbles along to the thunder. I'm keen to sleep, if only for my bedraggled day to find some formation, for dreams to move in and rearrange memory. The nights know how I feel.

XXII

It was 1968 when Aunt Lucinda went mute for a school term. She was fifteen years old. Apparently she wouldn't even talk to friends. Her mother, my grandmother Gaga, found a poem Lucinda had written, and took her out of school for good. It was a bold decision, but so was the poem. It was set in a forest's "cold bare hands," Lucinda holding a leaf that crackles and breaks. She sees the leaf on the earth in pieces and declares her own leaf is

> still holding out, though they've tried with all
>   their strength
> To crush me and make me fall . . .
> I won't I won't . . .
> I'll stay alone in the cold friendless world
> Striving for what I know is right.

It does sound a little dramatic. But after Lucinda was allowed to leave school, she won Badminton age nineteen. She would go on to win it five times more, on five different horses.

My fourteen-year-old self thought I should be a tennis player, even though I wasn't much good. It was around this time my stomach ache began, a sea-deep irritation I struggled to articulate beyond claims of a dysfunctional digestive system. It proved a mystery to conventional doctors, too, though not to my father. "You're just too tall," he said. "Your intestines must be too long."

Mum was also unconvinced. I presume she'd have sat up and listened if my diagnosis was death, but her daughter only had a tummy pain she couldn't see. She said it was caused, like her ongoing headaches, by frustration. "Keeping it all pent up," she'd say with a constipated expression. Maybe that was a subconscious instruction for me to be sexually free, a subject she wouldn't otherwise broach. Yet I was at my freest at that time, unrestrained on London's Friday nights.

My mother posted a strand of my hair to a psychic in Ireland, who rang five weeks later to announce I had anger and sadness in my belly. My London friends found this report really funny and began a daily inquiry as to the well-being of the monster inside me.

Time passed and Tummy Monster grew; their myth, my fact—until I learned to ignore it for long enough stretches that it became my myth too. People ceased asking. I suppose we think of pain as associated with an event—an accident, for example. We don't imagine it going on forever. I found no space for pain and its expression in daily life.

These were the years when teachers were seeking a "cause" for my disruptive activities, dispatching me to a learning-difficulty center where I was declared dyslexic. One teacher at my previous school had blamed my behavior on my tormenting siblings. "Are your brothers at home at the moment?" she'd ask, when I was in trouble or bullying a classmate. Then there was the woman who diagnosed me as a product of lifelong concussion. "I just think you've fallen off too many horses," she finished, as though there were a brainy soup spilling round my head forever trying to solidify into its original state.

Now that I've left, it just seems that high school lacked any potential for renewal. It went on and on, same days, same people, same structure, incubating me in my youth. I wriggled my way through like a caught fish, unsure how to demand freedom, wearing its mere look in my eye. I often felt like running away from home. But that would've made Mum worry.

By the end of school, my stomachaches had spread to my arm muscles and my head, as though an unlived life were occupying me. I fidgeted. I was never still. Freud does say that symptoms have the right aims but accomplish them in the wrong way. Was my body concocting plans to escape itself? "Aching to go" might have come into its literal meaning.

"I think you're just an octopus," concluded my brother Arthur one day. Octopuses' brains, he claimed, were spread across all of their legs. It's not even possible to think of their bodies as separate from their minds. Neither controls the other.

My pains are still with me as I ride the race.

It was also around the age of fifteen that I learned my habit of leaving. Still today I can't help slipping from parties without a word, and often I don't make it to them in the first place. It usually seems best to be absent and slightly missed rather than present but distant.

In Mongolia, shamans-to-be often fall chronically ill in their teens. The phrase for this can be translated into English as "illness from nothing." They're also prone to running off into the forest or showing other unusual behaviors. Their families hand them to an experienced shaman with whom they will spend years honing their powers.

When I heard about this shaman protocol after returning from Mongolia, I was a bit disappointed there hadn't been such a plan in place for me. I hadn't been singing to spirits or speaking to trees, but still, why did no one think to take me out of school and send me to a shepherdess or a lovely witch in a thick, foggy glen?

XXIII

"How you feeling, Lara?"

Kirsten and I crawled into the same world. I swallowed all truthful thought and said, "Great, you?"

That night, I'd dreamed of babies on horseback. Of diving into a mud bath and wrecking my head. Dreamed I was everywhere, and unaware. That I needed to take a friend to the pesto factory—we had all come up from the sea in a slow arc and were preparing to plop back in.

Can you carry on in the spirit in which you began? Kirsten and I knew nothing of how pain was spreading over the race field, dulling the resolve of riders who had set out to win—their pained bodies begging them to admit how little the competition meant in real terms.

The Derby had opened in a burst of energy, as so many "events" do. There was an exuberance to our meetings ahead of the race, but after start camp we had few chances to alter our impressions. Each person was like a book I'd only seen the front cover of. Devan remained, in my mind, Simply Ambitious; Todd was Simply Carefree; and Natacha was Simply a Chatterbox.

Who knows, maybe some of them still had me down as Simply Befuddled—the version of Lara who asked if we might please load each horse into a van and just drive our way round these 1,000 tiresome kilometers. Later, Clare would caption a photograph of me as "Totally on another planet," and Sandra, the French rider, would gawp when she heard I was ahead. She said it was dishonest of me to wear a veneer of hopelessness at start camp when my essence was raw ambition, as if I were some kind of pool shark.

Kirsten and I were getting no more than a glimpse of one another. The race was condensed enough that no one needed to deal with long-term me, as sister, daughter, mother, lover, or friend.

Some of my impressions of other riders and crew members would change when I heard stories afterwards. I discovered that my dream lover Adam had actually thought the race far too competitive. I read all of Richard's books and discovered the extent of his jockeying brilliance. As these snippets fell into place the race re-created itself in my mind. Apparently Monde's reputation as a horse whisperer traveled down the course, which lead to excited herders giving him increasingly difficult horses. He connected with and mounted each one. Monde was interested in the Mongolian way of relating to horses, and had said, at Start Camp, that he was racing to learn, experience, and win.

Of the thirty riders in the group photo at start camp just over half would end up at the finish. The others would fly home or return to the city early. During the race I rarely stopped to think about where each of them might be. I was wedged in, damming time.

It's the morning of the fourth day. I'm knackered. I feel farther from the finish than I did when I began, despite our being 350 kilometers closer. Kirsten's presence tames the day—humans are such absorbing distractions—but I can't summon myself to speak anymore. Words feel like an insult to truth (then again, even on life's bright days I feel as though I'm throwing meaning into darkness when I speak).

Outside, the sky is low and camp is cast in gray lake-light. I lift my saddle off the ground. It's supposed to be lightweight but my sleepy arms think it weighs more than a horse. Last night's dreams filter through me as I walk to the pony's open morning eye and whisper hello.

We're just about to leave when the lady of the place hobbles over from the top ger and points to the white sign in her fingers: *30 USD*. I look back up at her face. Her bun is tightly tied, stretching back the wrinkles from the high points of her cheeks. She shoves a handful of objects into our hands—the key rings and shoelaces Kirsten laid on the door mat as a thank-you to her. At start camp, word had it no one would accept money on the steppe, only gifts. But the lady is shaking the sign, stone-faced. By steppe standards, the price is steep. Neither Kirsten nor I have that much except in emergency money.

I try to produce my old smile but the lady's expression won't soften. I walk ten steps to the pony. He holds still as I climb onto his back. We sprint away with Kirsten and jump off ten minutes later at urtuu 9. 7:13 a.m. The vet listens at the chest of the pony, who lets me lay my arm over his neck.

Richard is leaning against a white picket fence outlining the ger, cloud-light shimmering on his forehead. I tell him the pony was really fast and jumped all the gorse bushes so I named him Steppe Orchid after Desert Orchid—Dessie—Britain's favorite racehorse in the 1990s. In the moment, I've no idea it was Richard who steered Dessie to two of his Grand National victories; my choice of name is coincidence. Richard gives nothing away, moving on to talk of Devan instead.

"She didn't make it to urtuu ten last night. Must have camped out somewhere between here and there."

I laugh this statement away—too solemn, too much the point. I want to be uninterested in Devan. I stand back to take in Steppe Orchid's head for the last time. Did he arrive in the world with all that love in his face, or has it fallen into place over the years?

Four horses stand on the line, unready, untended, almost free. Not knowing where the rest of the herd has gone. The herder says they ran far from the storm last night.

Maggie the steward approaches and insists we have breakfast. In the ger, we eat slowly, like long-necked dinosaurs. The breakfast is fish from the lake. Fish is supposed to be poor man's food—water mammals and fish are the lowest form of Buddhist reincarnation—but I find it delicious, and I love the damp smell. Maggie explains to Kirsten that the lakeside camps now attract tourists from the city, hence the lady's expectation of payment at our night-stop. I feel stupid for having been unprepared for this and for failing to predict how our lack of language might cause messiness of this kind.

When Clare and Chloe stumble in, I face my food. We say nothing about leaving them behind last night. Maggie reads out a message from the race chief in Ulaanbaatar. "Keep going, girls. You're closing in."

Richard catches me laughing as fish flesh falls from my lips.

Mouths grind. Minds boggle. A message from the outside world—I haven't thought much of it. They want a more competitive race, but not with a giant leap could we pass Devan Horn right now.

What is she like again? Sometimes she falls out of her stencil in my head.

A few minutes into the meal, Clare begins sniffling at my side. I see tears rolling down her cheeks. I'm bemused. Maggie tilts her head sympathetically, so I screw my face into a concerned ball.

"What's wrong? Are you OK?"

"I'm fine," laughs Clare through her tears.

"Why the tears?" asks Maggie.

"I don't know." She laughs again.

Being naive, I believe her. Aren't we all crying with glee to have made it so far? That's just how I feel. If I had Winnie-the-Pooh in front of me right now, I'd scribble, *How the fuck did this happen to me? I'm doing so bloody well.*

Don't swear, daughter, it's not ladylike.

So there's a lack of horses, Clare is crying, and the clouds are close to landing. I slip out to the resting ponies and jump the picket fence back and forth while I wait. Neither Clare nor Kirsten is ready. They're moving slowly this morning. How often we treat this ordeal as a race seems to be up to us. Quickly Chloe is on. We release our reins, yelling "Catch us up" to the others as the ponies hoist us away, galloping down onto the heaths by the foggy lakeshore. Richard's jeep roves the cliff above. I feel the silent clicks of his camera slicing us up into rectangles.

I want to rein the ponies in to preserve their energy. Chloe disagrees. If we fight with their heads and necks when they're keen, we can unbalance them. So, faced with terrifying speed, we find ourselves at our most relaxed, letting the thunder whip through us. For forty minutes we bolt into mists, we to whom nothing else matters.

On the lake's northern shore, my cream-colored pony launches himself over a puddle. He is airborne for seconds, heart hurtling. Chloe yelps from behind, thrilled by the jump.

Eventually I ask her about the matter on my mind. "Why was Clare crying, Chloe?"

"She's cracking."

"What do you mean?"

"She was miserable last night."

I shiver a little, relieved to be away from Clare. I find emotions contagious, swear I can catch them like flu. I've always been wary of upset and sickness. Aged seven, I dubbed people crybabies as though it were a life sentence and I winced in repulsion if someone missed school for sickness. I tried my utmost never to get ill and felt ashamed if I did. Although later on I faked sickness to save myself from days of school, I still had no empathy for the unwell and the upset. Clare has revealed the emotional hold the Derby has on her, and this has lodged me in a state of sickened shock. It will not occur to me to imagine how she might actually be feeling, or how I myself might actually be feeling. Such is the strangeness of my selfishness.

At the end of the lake, the soum of Ögii Nuur draws us into her silence. Dogs roam the perimeter of town, corrugated-iron buildings line the open streets. The paint has been stripped away by incessant Siberian winters.

Apparently the Soviets introduced the soums in an attempt to settle the nomads, but they had minimal success. Families tend to leave the soums for gers out on the steppe in summer, and some live out all year round. Now, in August, it feels as though a flood has swept through and carried life away.

On the soum's northern edge, Chloe stops for an emergency toilet break. I get off to hold her horse, who breathes peacefully into my hip.

"Is anyone watching?" she whispers up at me while crouching. It seems unlikely in such a ghost town.

"There's a crowd the size of a football stadium eyeing you through the slats in the fence here," I tease. "Hurry."

That sunless morning felt night-like, haunted, sinister. The wind grew wet and my pony tired enough that Chloe had to wait for us up a ridge. There was a dark cloud beckoning above her, and from that distance I got the feeling she could win, although we were still less than halfway to the finish line, with some unmouthable number of kilometers to go.

Chloe was light-framed enough for the horses to carry her easily but she was also strong. She had led us on my fastest leg yet. Now I'd be slowing her down. I was warmed by her waiting for me—separation didn't seem to have crossed her mind. I felt I'd entered an easy sisterhood, and for this I was unspokenly thankful. Many riders in her position, myself included, would've charged on without me, so used were we all to the jostling.

When I reached Chloe on the ridge, she leaned over to slap my pony with her spare rein. "Choo, choo," she told him, until we bowled on down the hill.

In the following hour, Chloe dismounted often to go to the toilet—often enough for my palomino to keep up.

"Think I ate too much fish," she yelled back at me.

Our pace slowed. I began imagining Clare and Kirsten catching us. Nothing is swift as thought—I felt it jumping through me. But riding in a big group just wasn't efficient. It was a simple thought, and when it came, I knew the race had me.

XXIV

Raindrops are tapping our helmets when we catch first sight of urtuu 10. The ponies march with their heads tucked into their necks, resigned to the weather. No one greets us. The storm has sucked everyone inside.

Eventually vet Helen emerges in a rain jacket that reaches to the ground. She speaks sentences simple and strong, moving her head certain as a bird. I tell her of the horse and the journey in a monotone, refusing to let the drama of the weather into my words. I want business as usual.

For noodles, I take to the ger. Chloe goes to the toilet again. The weather has given everyone an excuse to slow down. And what, exactly, has given me an excuse to speed up? I open the shutters to a competitor within me who sits uncomfortably with my self-image of a sideliner unaffected by the fray.

But our leader, she does need toppling. Somehow I imagine her with antlers now.

Plus, the pain. It goes down my arms and up my legs. I want to finish. I want the pain to leave.

When Chloe returns I assess her appearance. Her face is loosening. Her hair hangs wet and scraggly, falling out of the neat ponytail it held at start camp. Her jodphurs are muddy. Pooh to the pruned clothes and kit we thought would save us on the steppe. The weather isn't watching. Something other than Gore-Tex is now in demand.

The herder angles his hooded head upwards, wishes us well, and ships us off into the slanting rain. Matching gray horses trot us into hills that are neither high nor majestic, but plump and green. The wind blows in the grass and at the rims of our jackets. The ponies aren't fit but mine is faster than Chloe's. She shouts forth route instructions. Our main question is left, or right? Nearing the mountain range, we need a decision.

"I don't know, Chlo. Left's my lucky side. Let's go left."

On the path thereafter, I go quiet and fall into the canyon of my head. This is the mind-set where the world has no hold of me. I think I mastered it aged four in Mrs. Davis's music lessons. She called it daydreaming. Aunt Lucinda calls it being away with the fairies. The boys on the German exchange christened me Space Cadet. "You're all over the place," says Mum. Personally I like to think I can be terribly present.

Maybe it's fine to inhabit more than one space the rest of the time.

The storm undoes itself as we round the mountains. We're regaining momentum. I turn to find Chloe's figure gone again. Does she have a bladder infection? I wonder awhile. She emerges round the hillside with her pony trundling behind her.

"Sorry, just had to go again."

Chloe's complexion is ghostly. Pale skin paled, blue eyes iced—even when the sun bursts out and lends the land a post-storm cleanliness. The horses have not been enthusiastic about our voyage, but they canter occasionally all the same. We worm on through valleys of delicate wildflowers, their fragrance rising at our sides, the young sun and the old sky.

The climax of the leg came at a hilltop stop when Chloe threw up. Fishy matter landed with a pitter-patter. I heard it from ahead and thought, *Oh shit.* When she caught up, I was only concerned with the spectacle. "I'm afraid I missed it on camera. Can you pretend to be sick again?"

There were chords of pain in her laughter. Still, she took a mouthful of water and spat it out for my film. I made a note to suggest to ABC Alex that he use it in the opening of his documentary.

Dear Chloe, weak as water, stopped again on our next ascent. Her pony bent his head around to observe the dissolving lump riding his back.

"I can't carry on," she said. "Can we just stop for a while."

I waited at her side until the expected took place.

"You should go on without me," she said. "Go find Devan."

My innards were screaming for me to gallop away and clinch our leader. Simultaneously I was struck by visions of misnavigating and guilt at the thought of leaving Chloe in this state. She looked as if she were banking on the world ending before she did. In the stillness I could feel the winds of Clare and Kirsten on our tails. What was the point in standing there? Stasis felt so wrong.

I coaxed Chloe into standing back on her stirrups, where she braced herself for the sloppiest of canters. It wasn't elegant but it was motion, which was all we needed. Twice she sighed on the brink of collapsing and my meager response was "No, no, come on let's keep cantering."

I asked myself if sympathy was an art I had yet to learn or whether it was always an awkward, possibly ugly, thing, even when performed by experts. Chloe followed my hollow words until urtuu 11 was in sight, when her pony humped back into a short-strided walk.

I trot into the embrace of Pete the vet. Afternoon sun is lighting up his rounded cheeks.

"You doing really well. Really, really well."

He has not seen Chloe.

There's a congregation at the eleventh station, as though the neighborhood has heard about the race and come to visit—or just come to visit. The pony's heart rate is 64. Quickly I offer Oyuntuya, the interpreter, my usual line in English.

"Can you tell the herder I want to ride a fast-strong-wild horse? One who will bolt all the way there, one who is badly behaved." I allow the words out at a gallop without trying to sound too excited—I've been told overly embellished tones are suspicious in Mongolian. Though there are many different dialects, of which I might've heard only one, I never hear the language spoken loudly, and rarely with inflection at any point in the sentence—just a murmuring of throats, rough made smooth.

We all turn when Chloe slouches into the station looking sadder than the Grinch. She swings off her horse and lands like a slinky.

"Give me ten minutes" trails from her mouth as she disappears to the gers.

A herder from the Ganbaatar family, the creators of this station, bends his arms across his baggy deel, leans his chin on one palm, and presses two fingers against his lips. He walks up and down his line of horses and around their backsides before holding talks with a younger man. They unknit a chestnut from the line.

"Have you seen how green she is?" Pete returns from visiting Chloe and speaks at my ear. There's a note of gossip in his tone. "She looks just like the doctor did when I had to put him on a drip yesterday. She can't go on like this."

I'm keen to know where Pete buys his certainty. How do adults land on one voice and stick to it when all I do is accumulate them, my original voices multiplying whenever I hear new ones? Tomorrow I'll be narrating the world to myself with a pinch of Pete in my voice.

"You should ride on without her or she'll hold you up," Pete finishes.

It's a relief to have a third party propelling me onwards, keeping me from feeling guilty about Chloe, who at least will now be under Pete and the Ganbaatars' care. I quake as I shift into lonesome mode, summoning the air around me for support as I run down to the line of gers and poke my head into two. I find Chloe lying in an empty third. She is placed centrally, appearing as an embalmed celebrity. I leave her be.

Outside, a boy with thin legs is waiting to take my backpack for water-filling. I follow him to the ger next door, where his mother muffles me with offers of doughy bread, soup, napkins, sweets. Her encouraging noises, her tentative smile. I accept only a handful of sweets. Yesterday I might have sat around for a meal, but now I bear what I'd like to call the "responsibility" of chasing Devan. My adrenaline is spiking. I'm ready to run away from my skin.

I put my foot in the stirrup to mount. No goodbye, no nothing.

"Your bag is leaking," says Oyuntuya, facing my back where my water pouch is.

I notice I'm wet but I'm too close to leaving.

"You can't go four hours without water," says Pete.

Back down on earth, I unzip my pack and pull out the three-liter bladder. It spews water. I look up, clueless. A young boy with blushed cheeks stares hard at the bag as though his eye contact might fix it. A crowd is gathering. It takes me a moment to realize this might be because I'm now the chaser of the leader. My body feels important, but I don't feel up to the task.

A message speaks out of Pete's radio: two riders are approaching the station. Clare and Kirsten. I duct-tape the hole and dash to the tent to fill the bladder a quarter way while Oyuntuya runs to her vehicle for a spare bottle of water. I'm grateful for it, knowing the bladder will run out quickly now.

When I pull myself on again, I see the herder from the Ganbaatar family broaden his face.

"Tell her this horse will get her to the next station in less than one hour."

I hear this translated by Oyuntuya and half believe it, envisaging time itself speeding up, even though each leg normally takes at least three hours. Below me is a sedate creature whose snoozing ears drop sideways.

"Choo choo!"

Pony peels off his sleepy shell. Lickety-split, the urtuu falls into the land behind us.

He's in tear-away mode. The wind blows hard and blocks our

ears. His legs throttle as if dying to catch up with themselves, hooves flattening thousands of grass stems a second. If I move my heels a millimeter he bolts harder, so I tense myself into stillness and focus ahead of his arrowhead nose. He's a madman awakened. I love it, him, his intention.

I carry a backpack of bottles and worries: follow the road to the Tsengher Bridge, cross it, and follow the river to urtuu 12. Do it in an hour instead of three. Alone. It sounds so simple in the abstract.

We cover the first 10 kilometers too fast. Stripes becomes the pony's name because of the white stripe on his forehead, but I'm also thinking of Stripes, the *Racing Stripes* zebra who doesn't fit in. That was the first film to make me cry; I watched it three times in a row on an airplane when I was ten. Stripes being bullied by the horses, Stripes meeting the horses at midnight to settle matters away from humans, Stripes entering himself into the Kentucky Derby despite being half the size of the horses, Stripes galloping into a tree in a race against the postman, splat. I couldn't get enough of it.

Meanwhile in the Ulaanbaatar control room, race organizer Katy posts a screenshot of our dotted map positionings, which I will not see until after the race. *There is a rather excellent battle commencing up front. LPP looking strong, closing in.*

Dots can look strong?

By the time the sun was engineering her way out of the day, the first trees of the race glimmered in the distance. I hadn't seen a tree since Ulaanbaatar, nor touched one since I'd left home. In my head, trees on the steppe contained livestock-pillaging wolves, but they also lent me the idea that I'd soon be properly out of sight—even of the broader landscape. Just alone, with my four-legged friend. No facial gymnastics needed for approaching photographers or passing herders. I began to find a focus I can rarely locate in real life. Some torch within me came alight—a need, not just to beat Devan, but to amplify my insides.

There was a road on the horizon line, a car droning by every ten minutes or so. Balanced on the back of a pony, I found the sight of machines moving round bends spectacular, even miraculous— the way they didn't lean. As we neared over the next half hour, I could hear each engine slamming by. Such speed treated the space as empty. What the shamans knew before the twentieth-century physicists was that "empty" space is teeming with particles and waves of energy, spirits and ancestors, histories and happenings.

Cars were what I had come from and what I would return to, but at school I already yearned, perhaps unlike my urban peers, for the time before tarmac began: when mud was truth and cities trampled by hooves and carts went dusty in summer, when you had to exert your body merely to get around—forced aboard a horse, or else onto your own two feet, to bare your face to the breaking sun and stream your cheeks through the air.

Medieval history was one of the only classes I could concentrate in. An era pre-concrete, pure horse. No guns, just the chance to pull your brother's hair out with your bare hands like Harald Hardrada did in 1054. I think the in-touch-ness of that past draws me. I remember getting obsessed at age eleven by a yellow T-shirt picturing a mountain of hay with boxers, underwear, and pitchforks strewn at its base, captioned *Country Girls Do It in the Hay!* I thought it was really fantastic. No civilizational distractions, just free bodies meeting at the earth.

Being on a horse pulls you out of yourself and grounds you in the larger land. "Plug in," Aunt Lucinda says, to get riders feeling the animal and earth beneath their seat bones.

XXV

At the road, a sign emblazoned with Cyrillic letters passes us into the next district. Some boys dissolve their soccer game and run towards us, dispersing like atoms. Stripes lifts into a gallop but a flint pile then forces him to walk and the boys catch up. They move in a silence broken only by the occasional shout. They're throwing stones at one another. Or at us. I hold on to my smile, not believing they mean to attack the pony and me until a stone lands next to Stripes's nose.

He swerves and trips away over broken ground as rocks drop closer, the boys behind us now, out of vision and more sinister for it. Their arms are small but they hurl the stones far. I cling on as Stripes tries to quicken but trips, the ground too rocky for him to outrun the boys. How long will they chase? We aim for the wood in a trembling canter.

When the rutted earth irons out, Stripes gains speed and we

reach the trees, where a fir branch big as a mountain brushes my face. The boys disband. The pony walks on his tiptoes through the maze of trunks.

The unwelcoming welcome of the boys on the plains felt familiar; long ago I grew used to my older brothers chasing me out of their games and calling me things. Shatra, a race organizer, says the boys were the kind of troublemakers one could meet anywhere. They might've noticed I was foreign and known the language barrier would stop me reporting them to their parents.

Although it was a game for them, the moment leaves me thinking of myself as a body somehow foreign. In what terms should I threaten myself the question, *Do I belong here?* I think of us as riders, but we're also brute tourists, and our synaptic coming and going may be problematic. On one level, we're simply an influx of mainly white Westerners.

I wonder what the herders think of the race. It must be a risk for them to hand over their horses, even if it means monetary income— their animals can be returned lame or exhausted, they can even go missing, and that may be why, as the race goes on, some will refuse when I ask for their fastest horses. Shatra says that despite the hard work, the herders tend to really enjoy being part of the Derby. They are excited to meet each rider—and I have felt this attitude of warm curiosity at the stations so far.

Meanwhile, I begin to realize I can divide everyone I've ever met into people who think I belong and those who are less convinced— Dad's friend who once announced, in his sundial garden, that I should become a nun, and his other friend who refers to me as Avatar. *Go to your planet, Avatar,* he signed off in the only email he has ever sent me. Honestly, none of the labels or names have much in common, which I take to mean I'm an anyone, just like everyone, living out my days in the nooks and crannies between the labels, appearing as someone different to each person I know.

There are ribbons hung on some of the firs. Later I'll see part of a car in a tree branch. Only in reading will I discover that each ribbon is a prayer to the tree's spirit, or at least a passing gesture, and that Mongolians sometimes place car parts in trees to ensure against breakdowns.

Stripes blows his nose at the torrents in the river. The corners of his eyes, which I catch sight of as his neck snakes this way and that, reflect the streaming water. I knead him forward with my calves and pelvis, pressing at his fear until he creeps onto the sleeping bridge.

On the other side, I look back at the water and feel the urge to swim, and for Stripes to plunge his frothy coat, but Devan is calling, *ding-dong.* We slog on. Later I will tell people I had none of my own desire to win the Derby, that I simply needed to stop Devan from winning. Yet mostly I am just going fast, as fast as I can now, and I've got no time to stop and question why I believe evermore in the speed. Maybe that's the trick of it—the race has got me going so fast I've lost hold of my ducking-out technique. Like an adult who gets a job and forgets how to play.

My father and his sister know the art of getting on with it. It's locked inside their DNA. "Just do it," says Aunt Lucinda—daughter of a military general who seems, somewhere since the onset of the commercial era, to have swapped his commanding lines for the Nike slogan—not forgetting her stockpile mantra for not-thinking, *Crack on!*

Just do it! and *Crack on!* can be useful, but when they lean in for crescendo—towards *success! victory!*—I'm not so sure. Will a life obsessed by driving onwards and upwards have been worth it?

A river runs blindly alongside our canter. Trees line the farthest banks. Are they birches? Poplars? Why do poplars like to grow in lines? Questions are my line of attack now. Answers, I've none.

The astral plain stretches away in sandy browns. It's vast enough for the whole globe to gather in. Should I stop riding and plant my hands in the earth? Declare something? My legs are stranded in stirrups, my mind in motion. This must be how it is, to be water in a river.

Over and over I check the GPS, squinting at the sunlit screen, zooming in on my god: the arrow that indicates direction. I look up after one study to see an inbound silhouette, which clarifies itself into a boy aboard a pony. He holds a stick the length of a fishing rod. Perhaps they're returning from herding cattle. We slow our horses to meet.

"*Sain baina uu,*" I say, a simple hello, the best I can do. I feel the sunburn on my face as I move my nose up into the human world. Lone travelers over long distances move inside silences, silences packed with unspoken thoughts and secrets.

We chatter. Not much sense is conveyed between my English and his Mongolian. Then again, even in English, I'm never convinced there's an easy way of saying what I really mean. What was the language in which I first spoke to myself, and how hard did I have to work to translate it into English?

He concludes with a cackle, and I with a snort. As I ride away I almost fall off with glee.

At five o'clock the suits burst out in London town. White stones appear in the grass and I hold watch over them as we canter, hoping they don't score Stripes's feet. We only left the last urtuu an hour and fifty minutes ago and already urtuu 12 is in our midst, though not in sight. All I see is a singular ger, humming at the center of a solitude made obvious by the oceanic plain.

Stripes drinks from the river, scrambles up the bank, and saunters over to urtuu 12. I lean back and gaze upwards, following the late sun's rays down to camp, which is home to the Gankhuyag family. In front of me is Harry, the serious vet from Scotland.

"Watch out, Harry, don't come near me. I smell like a dying sloth."

"Are you ready for the heart rate?" he says, peering out of tinted glasses.

I trot Stripes up, wary of my face again, and its potential expressions. Harry checks his teeth. *As though we have time for dentistry*, says Stripes, chucking his head back and forth in protest. No other vet has bothered with mouth inquiries.

When I hear myself telling Harry I can't stop to eat a meal, I'm alarmed by my rush. I ask him to take Stripes's heart rate again. He huffs, thinking I'm too early, but it's already 60. He moves over to assess the stock in the back of his vehicle.

"Do you want some crisps, Lara?" he asks, picking up an enormous orange bag and lifting out a singular crisp to crunch on.

No time for paprika chips, thanks, Harry. I'm after someone from Texas, have you seen her?

"Four or five hours ago."

Oh. I almost thought Stripes would zip us up to her side.

The herder recommends a palomino who is grazing in human quarters with his back twisted like a turfed wheelbarrow as he reaches, one foot forward, for grass at the edge of the ger. I remark that he looks a bit fat, but the man stands firm—this is one of his old racing steeds.

Minutes later, he windmills his arms towards a set of mountains and I climb up and into another departure. 5:45 p.m. If last year's race length is anything to go by, Devan will cross the finish line in three days and two hours' time.

XXVI

If a rooster crows on a cloudy day, the sky will soon be clear. If a rat whistles before it goes into its burrow to hibernate, it will be a warm winter. If a chicken stands on one leg in winter, there will be a strong wind. These are three things I will read about animal habits here, once I've left.

The ground is teeming with singing hamsters. They dash away down holes ahead of the pony's hooves. The bigger holes must be home to the marmots, though I never see them. They tend to come out in autumn, fat from summer, or so says my book on steppe wildlife. I imagine them rolling across the hillsides like fluffy footballs.

Uuganaa Ramsay's father has a special outfit for hunting marmots. He wears her mother's old white dressing gown, a sun hat, and cream-colored shoes. Out he goes, waving a stick with a fox tail on it, walking on his toes, uttering marmot-like noises. It is beneficial for one's health to swallow a marmot's lung while its body is still warm.

◆

We remain on the same plain I entered last leg. A plain so vast it would be silly to carry on thinking we matter. The family at the urtuu we just left lined up to watch us gallop away, but we've since slid to at least six halts at river tributaries. I can't work out how to navigate around the water so my new horse has to plunge on into each one, bringing my ankles in with him.

A rider fifteen years my elder will later fall off in one of these rivers. Alex Embiricos is her name; it is printed in loud capital letters on the back of her helmet. I also recall strips of yellow on her clothing, a strength in fluorescence. At start camp she saw I'd forgotten my toothbrush and gave me one of hers. She had a tendency to hug competitors she had only recently met—including Dylan, the broken-ribbed South African she's riding the race with. Dylan is also about to fall off, a gaffe that will force him to walk 8 kilometers in search of his pony, Custard.

As we take up the ground, my horse tests it. Real bog in disguise or just boggy? Heavy current in the water? Deeper than it looks? Flints underground? Aunt Lucinda is in favor of letting horses work things out for themselves, rather than riding them on strides we've calculated for them. I'm a mere passenger at this point, surrounded by a thousand sounding streams.

There's a bridge 24 kilometers away we're meant to aim for, but maybe we should forget it. The horse could probably swim across the direct route. Mongol cavalry had saddlebags made out of cows' stomachs, which inflated during river crossings to help keep them afloat.

◆

The map book says two women at the next urtuu are Olympic judokas. I stretch my mind away from the steppe to imagine them fighting in an Olympic ring, having flown there in an airplane, and begin to find it surprising that I flew here myself. Like any human, I'm a traveler, but I'm better suited to the gradual pace of footsteps and hoofsteps than the leaping motion of planes, which severs me from the land. I wonder if fast travel dilutes us somehow—we the Everywhere Generation, making ghosts of ourselves while young.

In the months after the race I will have recurring Mongol Derby dreams. I write each dream down and let the collection fascinate me. One re-creates start camp, with the feeling of Mongolia mapped onto my home village of Appleshaw, where I fluster through dank cupboards in search of the old bungee rope. Another takes place in a dark moonscape, and another runs through Salisbury Plain. In one dream, we riders prepare and wait in an old Welsh house—lots of rooms, horrid baroque, long misty lawn, saddles lying dead.

My dreaming mind is never quite able to re-create the Mongolian landscape. Yet I want to tell the story from out here, not back in Britain. Here, on the steppe, is an orientation that tears apart my mind map. It breaks the spell of space and family.

Clouds are fogging the mountains and cooling the air. I throw passionate glances at my watch, which has resumed service. I must make it to urtuu 13 by 8:30 p.m. When the bridge rises to meet us, I'm flummoxed by its condition—gaping holes on the left and the far half falling down—but I saw a little car crossing it five minutes ago happy as a mouse. The pony marches over boldly, allowing his gaze to fall down the holes where water dashes westwards. It must be raining up in the valleys.

The clouds are charging in as though there's a sight to see in the soum ahead. We waltz round the town's edge, past a tower and a petrol station. The map book says Battsengel, this soum, is a good stop for ice cream or Coke. I see the town as a temporary measure, a pause in a thunder roll. It is free of sound but for some barking. I imagine men drunk at tables inside after a summer's day of airag consumption, but maybe they're out on the steppe instead. The tin roofs flap and the growing winds leave the land all shifting, all wandering. Only 13 kilometers to urtuu 13.

It begins to rain. Every drop is a touch of *here*. Here you are, on this baseless barren plain. My skin forgives and forgets each drop until there's a stream as relentless as the race itself, no distinguishing between the borders of my body and the downpour. Pony, I'd prefer your waterproof fur to these slippery sleeves.

We pass a camp where women and children wave, buckets swinging from their hands. I think to myself that it looks like home. Wind and rain continue filling the plain. The weather whips my concentration away; for fifteen minutes I fail to check the GPS as the horse pushes our bodies across the trappy floodland. I look down to see we're too zoomed out on the map. Pants. These tracks are wrong—they're sending us out to sea. I am stupid and cross for it.

I'm so used to spearheading forward that every stride back clicks double on my nerves. Then our path loses track of itself and we meander, searching for any path at all. Perhaps the riverbanks have burst. Something about the land seems to have changed, but I will not know to call it a "flood"—and give it the status of an event—until tomorrow, when a vet asks, "Did you get stuck in the flood last night?"

Mongolian myth has it that the world used to be submerged in water, us all a boundless ocean. In a nearby cave 2,260 meters above sea level, stones bear the imprint of sea creatures and marine vegetation.

It's a cross-section cutting sideways into the past. Looking back, I will see the Derby in such a cross-section, layered onto my London, Appleshaw, love and other lives—all mixed up, inseparable.

I don't know how long all this is taking, but I sense it's lasting. I feel the evening flowing to the end of the year and back. A jumble of lines on the GPS have recorded our movement. We're lost.

I call us "we," but he's the soldier, hooves on the line. Maybe I should let the reins go and ask him to take over entirely.

So where are we now? And where are we going. Home to Neverland?

Does it matter where we're going when we have no idea where we are?

I look down at my watch. Just twenty minutes until the 8:30 p.m. cutoff. Tomorrow or next month, I will see the photos of this race and think I look very free. But I am tethered, tethered I tell you, on lines from A to B to C, and from C to Devan. If I was four or five hours behind her, now I'm at least six, probably seven. If the palomino and I keep meandering, Clare, Kirsten, and Chloe will soon reappear.

I search the sinking plain for somewhere to stay. The minutes pile up, answerless. I feel the world collapsing slowly, like one of my failed banana cakes. A hoarse laugh shovels out of my throat and I begin, for some reason, humming "Happy Birthday," the rain stealing each note. Then, as if it were all a lie, I turn to tears instead, sobbing a few breaths before reining myself in.

Once, when Chinggis Khan was lost in the Eastern Xia, his army tried to drown a town by breaking its dykes, but they ended up flooding themselves instead. Was it karma? There's an idea that the Mongols were barbaric and the Europeans were/are civilized, which is amazing given the latter were barbaric enough to win all the wars "civilization" demanded over the centuries. It's true that Chinggis Khan's soldiers sometimes wrapped people up in carpets and kicked them to death, but this was, I've read, a treatment reserved for nobles only. By what standards Europeans ever denounced him I don't know.

We trickle on back towards Battsengel and I still can't see a place to stay. I talk as though I'm on the telephone, yet I'm thoroughly alone. Only the bungee rope pokes her eye out of my backpack, offering the services she's been yearning to provide since start camp. Dear friend, I can't sleep out here. The earth is a river, can't you see?

In her research on getting lost, writer Rebecca Solnit found that to cease being "lost" you don't necessarily need to find your way, nor do you need to retreat or return. You can just turn into something else. Transform. Maybe the Mongols exemplify this: initially suspicious of walled housing when they arrived in Muslim lands, they eventually swapped their nomadic lifestyle for such homes, and married into the religion.

It will be helpful if you can pretend on your horse to be *cavalry*, wrote my friend Iona in an email before I left the city. I can pretend anything! I replied, pretending.

Travelers can go out into the world with their devices and prejudices intact to smooth their journeys. Yet, etymologically, a traveler is one who suffers, I think—or at least, one who works (*travail*). The traveler forgets she's going home, and forgets herself, too.

We are damp animals. Sleepy and thirsty. Submerged beneath the day. And then: alone on the plateau, a ger. Patrolled by men of many ages. As we roll in, relief settles my rising shoulders.

I'm about to swing off to ask if we can stay when I realize these are the people who beeped their motorbikes when we passed an hour ago. It is easy for me to place trust in strangers, but I can't help noticing there are only men here.

Before we are close enough for them to welcome us in, my instinct overrides my need to sleep. I tack the pony and we trot away into the falling dark, minutes to go until the cutoff time. He braces himself beneath me. Thank goodness he burns so brightly; I'm deadweight at this hour.

The rain slows near Battsengel, where we find another camp we passed earlier. A little girl splashes over in a pink dress. When I get off she turns and runs, her plaits flapping on her back, and returns with a teenage girl who seems to say I may stay. I grin and find it hurts.

The girls eye the pony and me as we walk to the gers. He is my steed and we are a package; around the world your horse is often seen as a reflection of your character.

Beside the ger I reel out my evening word, "Tsütsan." Tired.

The circle of faces around me understands what I say, and that understanding awakens me a little, except for my feet, which went to sleep hours ago. My legs are carrying them as you would carry sleepy children. I lead the pony to the lines, where two men take over. One has hunched shoulders, the other a rapid, limping walk. I wish I could greet them with something proper like "I hope your cows and goats are fat."

When I ask where the toilet is, the teenage girl giggles. I ask again and she sweeps her hand through the night, nothing but darkness at the ends of her fingers. She leads me out onto the plain until I understand I should go anywhere, so I squat while she stands and we both cock our necks up to scan the sky, dark indigos mining the spaces between the clouds. At the bottom of the sky is a singular line traveling insistently sideways. It marks the beginning of the mountains. I watch them awhile, intent on the giant secrets sitting behind them.

For me, newly arrived and soon to go, the steppe is sometimes romantic. But later I will think back to the girl next to me and ask myself if it's monotony for her. I write about my own little path, but what about people I meet such as her? People less transient than I am. I wonder whether she would recognize any of the Mongolia I have written about. How many possible Mongolias are there?

Other than for conquering (territorially, economically, or psychologically), I'm not sure why we ever try to get an idea about countries as a whole. We find our own countries too complicated to define, and that must be the truth about other countries, too: imaginary and secretly borderless, they bleed into their neighboring seas and lands, impossible to fully catch.

I suppose we can all be prone, at times, to trapping certain countries in their distant, exotic pasts, ignoring their presents. I pluck out stories from the era of Chinggis Khan, but what I should really do is relinquish the authoritarianism of this narrative and ask everybody I meet what they think of the Khan today, or whether they think of him at all. Without speaking decent Mongolian, I haven't a hope.

Many history books in the West build him out with facts—a boy, born around 1162 to a humble family, who grew up to unite the nomadic tribes of the Mongolian plateau before conquering huge chunks of Asia and China, creating what would become, by the time his descendants expanded as far as Poland and Vietnam, the world's largest land empire. At their peak, the Mongols controlled between 11 and 12 million contiguous square kilometers, an area about the size of the African continent.

Later I will read of how Chinggis Khan is as much an ancestral spirit as a historical figure in Mongolia, the statistics no more important than his lineage and presence. He's the patron of the nation.

I hoist up my itchy trio of underwear, shorts, and jodhpurs, smiling the stranger smile. We lumber back to the gers. It's raining again. Each step I take costs me. My muscles and ligaments have retired, their goodwill abused by racing. They cling to the driftwood of my bones. There are layers of grease in my hair and on my skin. I dread my eventual cleanliness like I used to dread the start of a new school year.

The teenage girl, whose height I share, is talking with cheer, channeling absolute concentration into her few English words. Muddy striped socks peek out from her blue sandals. She says her name is Balorma and I say mine is Lara, doing so with all the enthusiasm I can muster—but the conversation dies down. I find I'm limited to one impulse: riding horses out in certain directions.

When we pass the pony on the line, I send him a sideways whisper. *I've run out of words.* His mane is bowed down towards a puddle. *You are grieved this evening,* he replies.

Inside the ger, I am rescued by my body. It quiets the flight of my mind as it drops, horizontal, into bed. I listen to the rain and watch the ceiling, where shadows of the fast-dying fire are playing. The grandmother murmurs to the baby, lullabying a little. Wrinkles route their way around her face—years of hard work and weather.

I wish I could talk to her or just sit with her but my eyes are reeling me into sleep. I feel I'm a goose who's meant to be migrating but can't be bothered this year. About to snooze forever instead. The smell of butter, dirt, and horsehair drifts off my fingertips.

Dear Ma,

I'm not yet halfway. . . . I feel a bit sick knowing there are 513 kilometers and many days all still untouched. In the morning I will leave behind a pink shoelace and a retractable clip, apparently sought after. Kirsten gave me a supply since I have no gifts of my own. I'm not sure who will wear the lace. The girl has worn only sandals. Perhaps the boy can wear pink. Maybe they don't have gendered colors here. I hope so, for the sake of the shoelace, for the sake of color.

No one will forget how you dressed my brothers in pink until I was born because you wanted a daughter. Didn't you carry on putting Arthur in dresses even after I arrived? Maybe I wasn't much good at wearing them. I must've been a tomboy, though no one used that word. I cut my hair to match the boys and tried to join their games in the darkened attic. At six I learned the trumpet, the farting noises of which delivered a pleasing headache to all. Subtler gains away from their realm included riding lessons and a hamster I could care for, gifted by you.

Deep into my hatred of pink, I never considered the search for a sister in between my brothers. I only felt someone missing when we were all together and wonder now if she was an imaginary sister I'd suppressed or let run off.

One day this year after I've been away a long time, you reach out of a car journey's silence to mutter you think I'll end up in Ireland. London looks to be crying through the rain-dropped windows. Conversations like these tend to take place in cars because I can't catch you still enough elsewhere. Like Lucinda, you're often in that hurry-rush—what for, I don't know. Even when my legs were short you never adjusted your pace. I had to trot to keep up in Sainsbury's.

Ireland, Mum? I protest your placing. In country psychology, Ireland is your category for the confusings. You tell me you wouldn't have wanted me any other way, but I know that means you're aware of other ways for daughters to be. Perhaps you wish I would brush my hair more or run closer to your social circles.

I guess we're not alike. But we bridge our gap by laughing breathlessly and muttering "It's fiiine," by talking to the hearts of horses and, back in the day, doing the wellington-boot race, too. How we trained for that race no one else gave a toss about, Gaga's old boots slipping on and off oh so well. My. Competitive even for the silly occasions.

Turns out my attempts at training for this race have been of little use. I've steadily been getting faster, relying on the Derby to teach me as I go along. This evening though, I got completely lost. Whenever you and I used to wander bogs or empty paths, my main sensation was calmness, even and especially when we'd lost trace of where we were. You seemed blissed out by disorientation and I learned to respond to it in the same way. Tonight, though, I just cried instead—the same tears as when I'd lose you in the supermarket. I know when we're at funerals you rub our backs and remind us it's good to cry, but alone in the middle of nowhere, it felt so daft.

Travel writers return from journeys abroad to write of their movement from location to location—naming each place, describing each path—but I question whether foreigners ever really know where they are, or whether our journeys are just stumbles through dis-locations.

You also say it's good to laugh, but laughing alone feels wrong too. So I lie on the bed like a blank-faced bean, flattening my emotion. Dad, your solid man, might be proud. Ma, you are being silent again. Is there a spirit standing on your toes and muting you?

Chloe's illness is really doing the rounds. Maybe I'm immune thanks to your Reduced Section raids in Sainsbury's. It's penicillin, you would say, as we spat out the moldy food weeks later. It's fine, you would say—good for you. We didn't believe you but we didn't not believe you. Maybe it made us resistant?

Maybe you made us resistant.

Speaking of which, isn't it disappointing that

my resistance has always revolved around really futile matters—teachers, etiquette, Mongol Derby positioning. Why can't I get angry about the sad news in the papers? Seems I have to be able to see it and touch it, and then I can't resist resisting it. Like when the headmistress went tyrannical and we donned long dresses to act out a slapstick version of her downfall. Pitiless, pointless, my favorite day at school.

The steppe escapes such London memories. I know there are quotes that tell you happiness lies within—"no need to search outside"—but I must've needed to come here. Like the ocean you so love, it's a land open and bare, a land that lets me be.

XXVII

What if my horse goes missing overnight? I have a premonition that he will. Deep in sleep I'm scared of such news. My mother's habitual fears are not dissimilar, cast in dreams of escaping chickens and flailing children. She's watching the race at home and growing unwell.

For the chivalrous in medieval Europe, and maybe for Chinggis Khan's soldiers too, "bravery" was equated with acts of strength. Back home in the car with Mum, I said I'd keep riding if I were to break my collarbone.

But my real fears aren't the broken bones or the missing ponies. My real fears are long-term affairs like school, marriage, and jobs. Anything requiring a commitment longer than a ten-day race. Maybe because millions of people manage these commitments, they go unnoticed. Ordinary jobs and relationships—spread over humdrum time—are rarely thought of as brave or strong.

And *How brave*, people will exclaim at drinks parties back home, *to ride across Mongolia alone.*

Three and a half years down the line, kind people will write cards saying *How brave, how tough you are* when I undergo a summer of chemotherapy for Hodgkin's lymphoma. I'll find it hard to reconcile the word "brave" with simply living through the disease life has given to me. Bravery won't feel like a choice. And what does "tough" mean? That I won't cry? Because I will, through London streets, up and down the swimming lane, around the fields of Appleshaw. Spreading my salt like a combine harvester.

XXVIII

It surprises me that the family has taken me in with such ease. On my journey I never hear, *Sorry, no room in the inn.* I guess I wouldn't turn down a lone visitor at night, but in the parts of England I've lived, people don't seem to come knocking. The gers have always been a network of support among rural Mongolians, who are often traveling around the steppe themselves and need places to stay. I presume this latest family is used to hosting passing anyones, from foreigners to shamans and prophets.

Molon Bagsh, a traveling prophet born in 1768, is still a household name in the Buryat region. He used to park his ox and cart and wander up to gers in his shabby clothes. People would take him in out of pity and look on as he settled by the fire, spread his hands over his face, and began spewing about the future.

It is said that as Molon Bagsh sat in each new ger, he found himself bestowed with a series of visions. I like to think that his placelessness, his lack of attachment, lent him the freedom of mind to receive these visions. And if bewilderment helps to bring up intuition from the unconscious, then perhaps there was nothing more bewildering than a new home or landscape every day. Shamans in Mongolia sometimes foretell the future by interpreting the cracks that open up in the shoulder blades of burnt sheep, or by reading the changing sky.

Well before the appearance of airplanes, Molon Bagsh predicted that metal birds would fly in the sky. He envisaged iron snakes encircling the world a few decades before the Trans-Siberian Railway, or indeed any other Mongolian railway. Spider webs, he surmised, would one day cover the entire earth—this transpired to be telephone wires—and abstract voices would be spoken into homes—enter the radio, some years later. People say the horses' feet he predicted sticking out of houses are the metal chimneys that came after his passing.

Some of his prophecies are yet to be realized. At the end of time, human bodies will be no higher than a person's arm and horses will be the size of rabbits.

Bagsh isn't the only known prophet—prophecy is a calling of its own in Mongolia, known as "future history" or "future talk." In a way it's just as important in the UK, where people predicting financial crashes are deemed sages. They merely replace the word "prophecy" with the sciencey-sounding "prediction." Prophets in Mongolia are often referred to as *üzmerch*, "someone who sees." Some of their predictions are listed in the newspapers.

One of the most famous of contemporary prophets is Dash-tseren, who began making predictions at the age of three. In the 1990s, his premonitions often made politicians uncomfortable. A year after he predicted one of the three state leaders would die, the head of parliament was killed. Dashtseren also foresaw a terrible disaster approaching the United States in the year before 9/11. He has even managed to locate oil in Mongolia where experts concluded there wasn't any.

"I do not understand myself," Dashtseren has said in an interview. "I do not know how I know things. Even science cannot work it out."

When I wake, there's bad weather inside my head. Fog rising, lost feeling. I think my head crashed through mountain tunnels in the night. For the first seconds of day I'm a train tricked into going the other way—rewinding, drawing back into darkness, tucking into the underside of time, delving out of the onwards motion to see what lies beneath, behind, around, and between. Deep inside I must be tired of the straight-knit line. Some force arrives to kick me upwards and leftwards. My dreams slip from my body as I bend out of the tent, bubbling short thoughts—the types you'd find in a washed-up goldfish. I raise my face to the cold and start surfing the day.

My fear wasn't wrong. The pony's not tied to the line. I've a career in fortune-telling ahead, I swear—until I spot him grazing on the near side of the ger. The men must have decided he was hungry. They've tied hobbles around his ankles to stop him straying off. I stare at him. When he curls around to itch his back leg, I think, *horse*, who formed you in a miracle? You lift your leg like a tent hook, light and free. You say nothing, yet in conversation with yourself, you fly.

Breathing again, I head back inside and haul into the morning ritual. Lift toothbrush to mouth, give up. Roll sleeping bag, stuff into cover; fail, try again. Remember how fighting men carried their equipment—horsehair lassos, cooking pots. Collect your torch. Shoes, can you really put feet in them, will you do it. Also, place soggy Winnie-the-Pooh diary in slightly less wet place.

Cherish the leaky blue sentences swimming through her soaked pages, because when the race finishes, they'll keep you out here at steppe. Earlier advice drops into ears. "Do not take your saddlebag off. Riders were bucked off last year when the saddlebags touched ponies' backs."

Methodically tighten saddlebag; wind rope around and around. Despise the iron discipline. I have no discipline. What gave me discipline? A journey of my own.

Outside, someone has retied the palomino to the line. He leans on his rope, dormant as a merry-go-round creature. The family has disappeared so I pick a toilet spot behind the ger and crouch. Not one of the nearby herd of goats lifts a head to consider me. Each is tearing her mouth at the grass with the zeal of a child new to an ice-lolly, yet this grazing business has been their work for years. It crosses my mind that if I were resigned to riding 140 kilometers every day forever, I might also be enjoying it more. It's the prospect of escape that turns the joy to agony: it will end. I could even quit right now.

I hope it ends soon. I hope the pain goes. I rarely think so overtly but such ideas swarm me unformed. Some scholars say the modern idea of hope only entered European history when trust in continuity faded, just before the Renaissance. In the race there's no jumping between scenes, no valley corner unseen. We ride continuous paths.

You are here on this earth forever. Nobody seems to tell you this.

Two men emerge and shrug goodbyes, tipping off the plain behind the pony and me as we canter away. I feel proud the pair of us has somewhere else to be. At last night's turning point, we find the flood still lingering and, far into the dead water, a crew camper van turfed at an angle. Its wheels are bogged down. I'm surprised to see a splinter of the Derby community out here on the water-sucked flatlands.

A skinny interpreter is slumped by the van's door, watching the vet and the driver scooping mud away from the wheels.

"We were marooned here last night," she says.

And did anyone hear me humming and crying?

As I ride on, the morning's low sky leans on the memory of my upset—as if to say, *Whatever was the matter, you old drama queen?*

The pony trots up a bog hill, stumbles down, and climbs another. I pause on the peak and see a line of horses wandering up a distant crag, their manes swimming on the horizon. Sky-mountains-river are all touching—hills streaming into sky and sky pouring river and something filtering through the clouds that looks so much like light.

What shall I do with my childish urge to tuck myself up in the land, to breathe and cry with the grass?

Racing is abominable. And the pony goes on beneath me.

At urtuu 13, I don't see any Olympic judo wrestlers. Only the vets are present and a bare presence at that, their swollen eyes straight from bed.

"Morning," mutters Kim—the tall blond one—touchingly unexcited by my arrival. They've only cleared three of the thirty ponies for riding. I stare longingly at the twenty-seven I can't have and allow a gray to be chosen for me.

Later Kim will tell me that on this morning I asked her to "find me a fast horse so I can catch that devil woman, Devan," although I don't like to think of myself as so explicit.

I lay my saddle on the ground to relieve my sore wrists and run to the ger, where I stuff my pockets with dried food, before sweeping back out into morning, still early, unlit. Back at my saddle, where Kim nudges my side. "Always good to see people from my tribe."

All conversation now strikes me as distinctly random, but this comment really forces me out to sea.

"Tribe?" I ask.

"We're tall," she explains. "Got to stick together or we get lonely, towering over everyone."

"Like sunflowers," I say, unsure where she's coming from. I guess I do grow out from a pony like a Christmas tree from a shallow pot. And perhaps I hold my shoulders as though I've never been loved. I walk over to the horse line carrying Kim's idea in my mind—I am tall and a little too much for myself, I am elsewhere. My soul has gone for a sprint in outer space and I am a shell, abandoned, gutted. Until I get onto a horse, or into a moment.

Olivier Costa de Beauregard, a twentieth-century French physicist, decided there was a four-dimensional world alongside us that was timeless—what he called "an elsewhere." It might be where my scattered bits gather. Or else the physicist was talking about the world that shamans journey to for their spiritual work. Maybe all physics theories are, in one sense, just new descriptions.

Kim and the other vet, Tom, watch the gray buck and bolt me out. What is so enlivening? We're no more than two creatures moving as one tiny sound.

Turns out they think I might overtake Devan on this leg. I'm unaware she slept at the urtuu with them last night. She's only an hour ahead of me.

184 · LARA PRIOR-PALMER

◆

The gray horse and I urge forward, parting the air as we go. When will we veer off course? As I watch the old centaur shadow mowing along at our side, I tell myself the route comes easily now. Mud snarls beneath the perfect grass.

For two and a half hours my focus is whole. He moves fluently and I note the quiet warmth of his company. You make no eye contact when riding, but we're in communication, working a shared form like shoaling fish. Horses have always been siblings to me, pressing their noses against my back and breathing out winter breath, slowly trusting. From his silence and the morning I draw something, something like strength.

The bad weather forges ahead, divinity on the move. The place we come to feels near an edge, as if we're about to fall from a person's chin. Instead of loneliness, I feel loveliness. Everything in the hour is familiar. The pony hurries on beneath me, persuading his way into my heart.

At the farthest pitch of an undulating plain, we meet gray slabs sticking up from the earth. *These are deer stones from Karasuk times four thousand years ago*, offers the map book in the tone of a sightseeing tour. I don't bother to admire these Bronze Age stones, nor do I note their ability to live so comfortably idle all these years, but when I read about them later, I am endeared by their not-seeking my attention. I look back certain that if you were searching for ways to fall in love with the world, to hug it deep and clean, you could do worse than drape your form over a stone and listen seriously to its silence.

Had we veered closer, we'd have seen the carvings of graceful deer on each plinth, their snouts elongated and their antlers swept back. Other creatures feature too—horses, moose, leopards, tigers—but none tame like dogs or cattle, perhaps because they don't retain the same spiritual independence.

We trot on towards a little boy perched on a big pony. His head leans into his chest, his eyes are large, and his grin wide. He turns to ride next to us until we near the gers of the fourteenth urtuu, when he trots an imperial circle and returns to our side, all the time talking. The tiring pony beneath me perks up and pulls faces with his horse. I watch them pushing their ears towards each other.

Do you find yourself searching for the meaning of life?

No, not really. I mean, what's the point when we're already full of it? You gotta live before you know the reason why, tralalala.

I follow the pony's lead, chattering and nodding agreement with the boy in some language beyond words. Researchers say communication among horses has barely changed over 45 million years and yet we humans, only a few hundred thousand years old, have already let our language divide into thousands of different tongues.

On the sign-in sheet at urtuu 14 Devan's signature is above mine, as it has been for the last three stations. I look at the times logged by the interpreters. She only checked in and out one hour ago. I thought I'd been reeling out again, but really I've been closing in. How my spirits lift! I berate myself for letting the news excite me. All said and done, I am yoked to moments.

Rumors about Devan have been circulating among crew members and competitors. They say she has packed enough American food to survive and declines Mongolian culinary hospitality. At urtuus she draws out fluorescent sachets and sucks the goo into her pursed lips. A friend from home has found her blog, which reveals she's sponsored by "pure, natural energy gels." Apparently, she calls herself Texan Temüjin, which is Chinggis Khan's birth name. It sounds like she's relaunching the empire in her head. My friend writes a message I will not see. *You are catching up with Devella Deville—if she doesn't scare you, no evil thing will.*

XXIX

Urtuu 14 lies at the westernmost point of the course. Now we head north, and later back east. Our route will draw an unfinished circle. They say the Olziibayar family has the wildest ponies of all twenty-five stations. The course organizers try to find them every year, no matter where they've migrated.

I barely pause at the station. The scent of mutton holds the air. Time for lunch? *Woof.* I'll wait. The mounting process is operatic. An old herder draws out a dark dun—skinny body, strong neck, black mane sprouting. The other ponies' manes have been bristly-short like toilet brushes. I think they chop them off the geldings. This one must be a stallion. Just like in the UK, the horsemen here tend to believe that the really important things—spiritual qualities, character, and stamina—are passed on by the stallions rather than mares, although that view is changing.

The herder grips the bridle from aboard another horse while his tiny son plants himself ahead to stop the pony from shooting off, bouldering his hands into its shoulders. Contact. I am strapped into my new home. The herder holds his bridle tight to his knee as we zip out onto the steppe.

Moving across a plain blanketed with sage, the old man speaks occasionally, though I don't know with what intention. What are we saying with our faces before we open our mouths to speak? All our delicate muscles, erecting, twitching, collapsing like tents.

His eyes glint and I trust him in this. As we shuttle along, he teaches me how to hold the reins in his way. It makes me think of all the sports and skills where masters teach you how, commanding until you repeat back their methods with ease—and maybe you grow hopeless in it, because you spit like a cross llama when someone tells you what to do.

This is a rare instance of instruction. No one has told me what to do since I arrived in Ulaanbaatar. I try to find sense in the old man's chants. I feel so foreign trundling on the earth beside him, and yet he brings me closer to a there-ness in the landscape, to the rhythmic cycle of seasons all missing from a ten-day race.

After fifteen minutes the old herder points me in the direction of a mountain and releases my pony from his grip. Beneath me a lion takes flight. When I look down at the GPS, the dun pony—whom I'll later call The Lion—steps up another gear, attacking the air ahead of his nose as though determined to blow out all the candles on his birthday cake.

The basin ahead is vast as an airport runway, traveling out in changing shades of brown and green. I expect us to pass through alone, although a dot—I don't know what—hovers in the hazy distance. It increases in mass while I tussle with The Lion, who is begging for a bigger gallop. What will we think of each other, scapegoats in the wilderness?

I've earned a semblance of control by the time the identity of the pink dot is clear. She's our leader. Striding towards us, horseless. *Well, hullo there, Devan Horn of Texas, in your hot pink Gore-Tex jacket, and your lime-green neoprene chaps.* This is the voice I imagine they'll use for the ABC documentary.

Where has she come from? Coughed up by the land? Hopped out of my ear? She's walking in the direction of urtuu 14, where I've just come from. I slow the pony as I shout through the wind, reminding my mouth that it is indeed a mouth. "Wow, are you all right?"

"Yeah, I'm fine," she replies.

The Lion is carrying me away.

She yells after us, "I'll catch up with you in a second!"

Given she's on foot, this is an amazing idea. Her tone is upbeat but there's no smile in her face.

Chloe and I were convinced we'd never see Devan again, so far into the lead had she flown, so convincing were her winning words at the outset. I think the herder—he was trotting leftwards at last sighting—must be riding after the pony she fell from. *It is easier,* goes a Mongolian proverb, *to catch an escaped horse than to take back an escaped word.*

We bowl on. The Lion wants to break into a gallop. I hold him in an oozing canter. On the spread of the steppe I've grown used to feeling like an ant making her way through honey. But this horse's movement is aqueous, the land doesn't resist him. There's a wholeness to his wildness and our going together feels prehistoric.

He is free from history, free from country; he doesn't care about the Mongol Empire, nor any empire.

For all the empires horses helped to build, and all the land they captured for us, what they really invoke is an opposing set of forces: fleeing, giving away, leaving behind.

In *The Tempest*, Ariel, a spirit, sings about a *sea-change / Into something rich and strange*. He's describing a transformation beyond recognition. With The Lion I feel reincarnated into some such something. I'd like to ride this leg on him forever.

We have a new leader, broadcasts Katy in Ulaanbaatar. It's freeing to be out in front, though somehow it hurts to celebrate. Soon I'm a fretful leader, certain I'm the next line in the Bottle on the Wall song. *"And there was one green bottle, sitting on the wall . . ."* I will accidentally fall.

Flashes of pink blink in my mind. I check for variations on Devan behind me. I'm sure we dart out of her sight at every corner. After ninety minutes we're at the foot of a mountain so enormous it must have made many a passerby scowl, but not The Lion. He insists on trotting up the steep, stony trail with his head held high. In every hoof-plant he punctuates the ascent, but the sentences he places in my brain are contrary to that power I see in him. *I am not energized by myself alone. I am married to the spaces we sail through.*

I'm wary of his speed and my luck. "Sit back!" Aunt Lucinda shouts at riders when teaching. "The most dangerous thing you can do is get ahead of the movement." Devan can't be the only rider to have pictured herself as leader. Clare, Kirsten, Chloe, Matthias, and Paddy all seemed to live in the hope. It's odd to think of them now, and of those who lent me their kit and lathered me in advice at start camp. They must think a miracle lifted me to this position. Myself, I can't tell what has happened.

The northern face is bright green. If eating grass were my habit, I would dine here. But The Lion harrumphs, showing no interest in the Michelin-starred plant life or in the water. Little trees lean off the mountain. He canters me down through them, holding his tongue while I lower my head and fall into his silence. How is he so merely himself? Himself in all his blatant being.

Baska the vet is casual, calm as usual. Only Devan-paranoia haunts my peace. I inspect the horizon beneath the mountains, questioning the woods in case she's disguised herself as a tree.

I cast a look to The Lion as he's led away to the lines. *Thank you for flying me, for bettering me, for allowing me.* But retrospective gratitude doesn't work with horses. You just have to behave according to the social contract while on board. Hopefully, I did. Fixed in momentum now, I don't pause long to think of how I'll never see this pony again. As I turn away my mind pulls a plug, which lets him leak through a hole. But shortly after I move on he'll still be somewhere, pushing the world around under his hooves.

One strand of Mongolian philosophy has it that my chest, not my brain, is the seat of my consciousness. It contains my *hiimori*, my wind-horse, an inner creature whose power needs maintaining. When you rub a racehorse's sweat into your forehead or ride a great, quick pony, you strengthen your hiimori and improve your destiny.

◆

In the ger I wait for water. Meats—body parts—hang from the rafters. Baska talks through the interpreter to tell me he's pleased I'm winning. Then I find him outside a minute later, puffing on his cigarette with detached passion.

At the beginning of every new leg, I notice the weather. This time there's sarcasm in the sky. I see the face of a very human cow staring from one of the bigger clouds. I am frustrated with the clouds, perhaps because I know they wouldn't react if I touched them. And they're so far away.

I'm slung onto an ordinary, hairy beast and it all feels like a chore again. My stomach is brittle. The Lion, my last pony, took me north after much westerliness. We've now turned east. I don't like going back the way we came, back towards the city.

After twenty minutes, the new horse and I come to a soft river where naked children splash their mothers and beckon for me to join. I eye the river up to where it folds back into the mountains and feel it hang from my neck. Water, darling water. My clothes are saturated in sweat but there's no time to stop. The children prance after us, screaming as we pace on up the hill.

Particles of Devan waft through the air. I check the land behind us. It's too much like a game of Grandmother's Footsteps in the garden, with all that pure young fear gripping me again. At school they really encouraged "creativity" and "imagination," as though the imagination wasn't a rotten thing in which you could ensnare yourself.

Miles of strides pass. My other main sentiment, besides a fear of being caught, is profound boredom. It may be a symptom of landscape ignoramia, which involves disconnecting from your surroundings. Lucy did say on the telephone, "You won't expect this, but you'll also get very bored."

"Isn't the steppe beautiful?" I'd said.

"Yes, it is beautiful, but after the first day you won't notice that. You'll spend every remaining minute checking your GPS."

Some people like a very boring landscape. A subtle desert, a half-hearted hill. Little rock there, little bush here. Little rock there again, little bush here again. A series of dull repetitions for anyone who takes pleasure in regularity.

Children never seem to remark on the view. It's as though they have priorities closer to hand—admiring the beauty of distance has no practical use. Maybe they also feel so much a part of the land that they wouldn't think to separate themselves from it in order to make comment.

I should take up singing to ease the boredom but there's no one around to annoy. I used to spend whole afternoons on the rocking horse in Appleshaw, keeling back and forth as I sang out the sentences from a random page in a book about Wales.

Mongolian ballads known as "long songs" are said to translate the contours of the land into verse. If the steppe had a tongue, these might be her sounds. Ariunbaatar Ganbaatar, a famous opera singer, says being with his family on the land is what gives him inspiration. "Wherever I am, the land is what I imagine when I sing." He grew up riding 100 kilometers a day.

By the time the sun suggested departure, casting thicker light on the highest mountains, the pony was tired of me. *Be off my back,* he snorted. Occasionally I slapped his shoulder for a canter and received a lapse into walk. The average speed of a Derby leg is 11 kilometers per hour. The Lion must've gone twice that fast while this next horse dribbled along at about 5 kilometers per hour.

We passed a camp of lonely gers and animals gone stale in the sun. The hills kept coming, rising like bread. The horse, who cantered on his forehand, descended each one in a sprawl. In the plains beyond, there were more carcasses than usual. Lives leaped from the bones and all the horses of history danced by my eyes.

I'd seen Devan toppled, but it hadn't relaxed me at all. If this was a game of Snakes and Ladders, I remained convinced, like every paranoid world leader, that I was about to slip down a snake.

Onwards I marched in the manner of a manic London commuter. I think this is the mode of my father, even in sleep. My, it must be painful to be pinned to the future. To exist in *italics*. In those taut afternoon hours, it was achingly obvious I was unable to live in the present like the pony, and equally unable to see into the future like the prophet Dashtseren. I was just stuck in the race's petty timescale. Perhaps most of us are stuck. This may be why people flock to fortune-tellers and watch the news—to hear out an extended version of themselves, to see further forward.

The dark backwards and abysm of time, says Prospero in *The Tempest*. If time was space—an abyss, a gulf—then what was space? Perhaps closing my eyes would've summoned my mind home. If I kept looking across those broad spaces, so many swatches of future at once and no solid objects for my eyes to cling to, I felt I'd go mad.

Perhaps somewhere, somehow, the depth of the steppe also reminded me of death, the deepest thing I could imagine. The lure of the abyss, and the danger of falling in.

XXX

Four hours of hot riding pass me by. With the sun trapped in my skull, I lead a knackered pony towards urtuu 16. Figures dwindle in the fold of the hills, Charles the steward at their center. He and I haven't crossed paths since urtuu 7 two days ago. Skeletons, mountains, and marmot holes hold the space between that day and this one, and the people from the early Derby have faded from my memory.

As we near, I can make out his hands resting in his pockets, his bottom sticking outwards, and his cap concealing his face. I like to think you can see inside someone's head from a certain distance. Barbara, a vet, fidgets beside him. Her hair is plaited back the French way, her red deel is draped to her ankles and rolled up at the sleeves.

"It's eighty-two." Barbara drops the stethoscope and draws back from the horse's stomach.

I gulp. So high.

"Did you make it canter when it didn't want to?" says Charles. His accent intensifies it for me.

"Have you had high heart rates before?" Barbara joins in.

"No, only my first horse."

Charles asks for my vet book, where records of fifteen horses lie. He peers over its seam at my heaving steed while I stand by, unsure where to look.

"This one is gonna take the full time to go back down to sixty-four. . . ."

The "full time" is forty-five minutes. The longest I've had to wait to date was Brolly's fifteen minutes at urtuu 1. I shrink into a prickly silence.

In the waiting minutes, Charles and Barbara let up a little.

"I love your accent," I say to Barbara. "Where's it from?"

She and Charles burst into laughter.

"I am from Belgium."

Her words float across the wind with loose wisps of her auburn hair. I withdraw my feeling for Charles, seeing him bantering so idly with her. Maybe he's just one of those trees who attracts bees. That's what I think when I start to feel something about someone. I'm just another bee, and my young buzzing has been heard before.

"Did you see Devan on your way in?" asks Charles.

"No, I overtook her on the leg before. She wasn't with a horse."

"Oh," he returns quickly. "She must have taken a different route from you because she came through here an hour ago."

"What?" I act out a shrug. "I probably went the wrong way again."

But I thought I came the most direct way. Foolishly so, perhaps. I can't tell how she has passed me without my even knowing. Jetpack? I'm awed by my competitor.

I move on to ask after the others, masking my frustration where I can.

"A bunch of people going home from urtuu nine today," replies Charles.

"Is everyone OK?"

"Yes. Adam, Alison, Paddy . . ."

"What's wrong with Adam?"

"Oh. He had . . . chafing . . . on his . . ."

Charles stops and gestures downwards, locking his eyes on me until I bend backwards in laughter.

For twenty minutes I walk the horse but his heart rate stays high. I have overridden him. This is true, true in a terrifying way, like a medical diagnosis. Charles takes over the walking and dispatches me to the ger to taste the vegetable sushi, which is a surprising dish after days of messy noodles. I munch my way through the pyramid of rolls, burying my stomach in food while the horse breathes hard outside.

A wide-eyed girl is watching me eating. I can hear Barbara's laughter erupting out of flirtatious conversation. On my fourteenth piece of sushi, Charles stoops into our silence and looks from the plate to me.

"What you done with the top layer of sushi?"

I blush.

Outside, Charles and I walk slowly. At his side, I feel the tightness in his chest, the challenge of being male. I wonder how he lasts inside that beard. The conversation leaps when he says Devan hasn't actually overtaken me. He's been playing with me? The cheek of it. So attractive. I feel silly for believing him.

"No idea where she is," he says.

198 · LARA PRIOR-PALMER

His eyes draw circles around me as I drop and laugh relief.

"Lara, you know I buy you a vodka if you win."

Is he joking again? He's stone-faced, and I am confounded. I thought he didn't care, yet he seems to have a strange faith.

Eight minutes before the forty-five-minute penalty time, my pony's heart rate comes level.

I ride a palomino out onto golden land. Bog seizes us twenty seconds after departure. His hooves sink between clumps of fluorescent grass and scramble on, falling from island to island while the light eases us onwards into the late afternoon. It's the type of light I notice at Christmas time. It suits the ends of years.

We're making our way over the fingertip of a hillock midway through the leg when I see Charles's khaki camper van bouncing in the distance and think, Oh dear, I've done it again, fallen in love, and found height in the falling. Evening slices it raw—the feeling that I long for him, and long to win the Derby for a new purpose: to impress him.

I can distract from this embarrassing truth with another reference to *The Tempest*. At the end of the play, Prospero begs the audience to forgive his magical deceptions, claiming the purpose of his project was simply *to please*. In the 1623 version it's written as *elfe my project failes / Which was to pleafe*.

What if I just wanted to win for myself, without wanting to beat Devan or please Charles or any other audience? It's a lonely thought; I wish I were strong enough for it.

My pony goes quiet as the ABC crew car charges out to meet us. I've taken us straight instead of right for ten minutes so we're behind time. It may even be nearing eight o'clock under this tangerine-lit sky.

I haven't seen the ABC lot since the rainy morning on the second day. My fancy for Alex has since gone extinct, replaced with my affections for Charles. Still, I'm excited to see him. Company. This sentiment vanishes when he begins question-flinging through his window, shouting things about my "being in the *lead*."

Later I will hear how last night, Alex had wanted to send Gloria the reporter out on a Derby pony at urtuu 9, but the pony escaped when she bridled him. He returned half tacked up with his legs thrashed, trotting lame. Alex asked to use another horse but the station was already short. He laid down his camera in protest and told everyone that one million people watch his show and that it is very important.

The seventeenth urtuu lies in the lap of a rangy plain backed by woodland. I moor my mind in whatever's beyond, the undanced spaces. I can see Charles squinting out from beneath his cap. He stands in front of a line of horses who drowse in the ethereal light. I climb off and walk the pony past the log fire towards him.

While Charles takes the heart rate, Richard roams calmly, quietly—a sorcerer undercover. I feel the precision of his camera in the chaos of the station. Crew cars surround the gers like oversize litter. Bodies in T-shirts pop up like magic tricks. Striding herders, delicately tripping children, aloof interpreters, and ABC Alex right in my face, talking incessantly.

Charles sets less of a stage here. As he holds the stethoscope to the pony's ribs in silence, I ask myself whether he might be irritated, perhaps trying to hide the fact that he's doing the absent vet's job. I am briefly shocked by my admiration for him and decide to imprison him in descriptions such as *inconsistent*, even *untrustable*. Yet my ears are still pricked in case he comes out with any more lines I won't forget, like that one about buying me a vodka if I win, which I somehow equate to us sleeping with each other.

At 8:09 p.m. the palomino's heart rate is still not level. With twenty-one minutes to go, they'll think me crazy to leave a station so late. Will you get anywhere? Will you find a place to stay? Doubt is king.

Alex carries on. "Laura, this rivalry with Devan: Is it a question of UK versus USA?"

My name has been punted about in many forms—"Lera," "Lora," "Larrah."

"No," I reply, "this is a question of UK versus Texas. The rest of the U.S. is fine."

That must have been enough to make it onto American television.

By thirteen minutes past, the pony's heart is cool but someone has spotted Devan tumbling off the skyline. I rush to choose a new horse. The ABC reporters bumble after me, droning on with their rhetoric.

"Laura is planning to ride out the station with just ten minutes to go." (Emphatic swivel of reporter's head in "Laura's" direction.)

"Laura, what *is* the strategy behind this?"

Before I can tell my tongue not to, I hear it saying, "I can't think of anything worse than spending the night in a ger with Devan, and you asking vacant questions through the tent walls."

There is a dodo's heart beating in my breast.

I can see my next horse behind Alex. He is bucking under a man from the urtuu's Byambasuren family. Devan rides in from the east, her calves sandwiching a well-exerted pony. The crowd swarms in on her while Alex stays with me.

"Wow, what's that? Laura, let's ask you one more time, why are you riding out with so little time?"

He's waiting for an answer. I give him a frustrated grin. "Because I don't want to spend the night in a tent with Devan."

Or I just like to run away, because somewhere I am terrified of people.

Devan appears on my diagonal. "Are you really planning to ride out now?" she says.

I bustle off, using the rush as an excuse. I'm scared to look at her in case she sets me alight. "Standoffish" is the word she will choose to describe me in her post-race interview, which I think is probably fitting.

8:17 p.m. Gathering up, I find my map missing. Disaster. But I'm into the theory that lost items are unintended sacrifices for some invisible good. I suspect the map has dropped out of my denim vest pocket, even though I don't really understand how things fall out of pockets—the gravity of it, and why an object would do such a thing as to fall out of a pocket when it was so happily in there. What's the need to escape?

I see Richard's camera looking at me and walk up to him.

"Richard, do you think I can maybe please have your map?"

He lowers his lens. I didn't know his face could make such a shape—as though a potted plant has fallen onto his toes. If my mind weren't cluttered with ideas of departure, I'd snatch his camera and capture his expression.

Ten minutes and counting. Like Aunt Lucinda in one of her hare-brained rushes, I run to Richard's car, ask Jagi, his bright-eyed interpreter, for his map, and trot back over to give him the news. "Richard, I've taken your map."

He mumbles, "But I need that to navigate between the next seven urtuus—"

His slight frown makes me blink.

"Do you want me to ask Jagi if she'll come with me instead?"

"No thanks, Lara."

"So can I take the map?"

I stand where I am. Power on my plot.

Thoughts pause in his hair. "No."

"Can I use it to wipe my bottom on too?"

8:21 p.m. I swing my sore leg over the next horse and we fly from camp, a spark released from the flame. In the falling dusk we rip round the mountains, casting off the plastic drama as green earth sweeps by. Every stride knits us further into the evening, until we feel night invite us in, alone, anywhere. I am fled, with Richard's stolen goods in my backpack.

XXXI

What is space? Here.
　　And where do we come from? No idea.
　　To whom do you belong then? Daughter of the land and sea?
　　Daughter of the land and sea.

The sun is setting behind us. Shades of orange and gray. Dark clouds roll around the valley ahead where three gers rest, a column of smoke rising from one chimney. As the horse draws us in, a lady with tender dark eyes walks out towards us.

It is 8:33 p.m. For twelve minutes the horse has galloped and galloped out of himself. Initially I couldn't see any camps on our path and I thought we might have to bungee-rope it. But here we are at a standstill only three minutes after the 8:30 p.m. cutoff, a smug 7 kilometers ahead of Devan.

One of these nights, my brother Arthur broadcasts that I've

204 · LARA PRIOR-PALMER

slept out in the open with my pony tied to my ankle. This gives the bungee rope the fame she's been so desperate for—and in months to come, I will field inquiries about the mythical night attached to my steed.

Myth's capacity to mutate is strong; in the years after the Derby, people will ask about "that trek across Madagascar" or my "summer riding a donkey in Iraq." Both of which, for a certain British psyche, may offer exactly the same story: *girl on erotic power-animal traverses the exotic.*

Race rules penalize each minute of riding beyond 8:30 p.m. with a two-minute wait at the penalty sitting station (urtuu 20), but I reckon they won't pick up on my extra three minutes. At briefing day I got the impression the trackers don't transmit very frequent signals. Even if I'm penalized for those minutes, it will only make a six-minute penalty, which, when I come to sit it, will be negligible— it takes me at least ten minutes to change horses anyway.

I lay the side of my head on my praying hands. I mean to ask, May I sleep here? I am a cauldron of my body's juices and tiredness has rendered me close to mute. May I come in? The lady's face broadens. She fetches her son and beaming husband to greet me, and we stand as a foursome in the tempered ecstasy of wordless conversation.

The pony and I saunter away for a drink at the river, where the water is quiet. The light has spread her pre-dark colors, those shades of dusk that match the temperature of dreams. We meander until we find a resting place in the reeds. I bend my form around a ray of the lapsing sun and feel all the day's motion leaking from my pores.

While the pony plops about the water, I stare at some faraway gers. Like a village in Devon, the scene might've been the same three hundred years ago, yet during that time, some humans have busied themselves with inventing things like electric lights, television, and the internet—bewitched by the promise of increased speed, of motion forever onwards, upwards, and never enough.

Have I been casting off chapters like a paper shredder, uninterested in anything but speed?

The sun has gone under. Up at camp I stand calm, watching the boy tie my pony to an iron rod in the ground so he can graze the night away. We walk slowly to the tent, where I don't know why I bother trying to explain to his parents that I'm riding 1,000 kilometers because—*please*, don't be daft. Why the extended expedition? What is the concern? As though the journeys of our lives haven't proven quite enough?

They do not recognize the name of the family whose station I say I'll seek come morning. They understand we're headed over the eastern pass, so I leave it at that and turn to the noodles the lady has handed me. Her scraped-back hair shines under the light from a single bulb, so much tidier than mine.

Opposite sits a man I think might be her husband. He eats, though she does not. The wrinkles in his cheeks move with each munch. We grin a little but say nothing while the wet noodles dangle from our mouths.

In the gers I tend to plonk myself down in any old place, but it is proper to sit in the south if you're young, the north if you're old, the east if you're female, and the west if you're male—none of which I'll know until later. Apparently the social form inside the ger is strong enough that people sometimes unconsciously mimic its circles when meeting in Ulaanbaatar's squared-out rooms.

I don't know what lovers do for privacy, given the lack of partitioning in a ger. Maybe if I wanted someone's company, we'd meet on the steppe at night.

I'm lying down for sleep when the son stoops inside. His legs bend like springs as he trips to the back of the ger and uncovers a television. It works! Well, why shouldn't it? The screen lights up his face, radiating his smooth cheeks. Four more family members file in to spectate while he changes the channel to Forex economic forecasts. We gaze at the self-assured presenter, who thrives inside the screen, spewing out numbers somewhere in America. When the boy notices I find finance senseless, he switches to a German channel.

From bed I try to concentrate on the characters on screen—wriggling fluorescent shapes—but my eyelids grow heavy. Minutes later I open them to the mother's face dangling just above me, moonlike. Her arms are laying an extra blanket over my sleeping bag, and the family has shifted their focus from the TV to me. A giggle passes around the ger, as though it's a very cheeky thing to be providing me with another blanket, or to be watching me as though I'm the television. I smile with my eyes shut again. They know not where I have come from, yet this is what they do.

It must be fully dark outside, though I've not seen night proper since day one. The sky might have unscrewed or the trees escaped their shapes, I wouldn't know. New moon, old moon, I wouldn't know. I hear the horse neighing shrilly, as though calling a star down to earth. Me, I want to be tucked up in bed at home, hugged all round, loved like a well-soaked teabag. But no, not really—that must be someone else's dream. It's just I haven't decided if I'm woodland-wild or fireside-tame, and probably I never will.

My mind mutters on as the music of a rom-com on the television whirs. Oh my I'm ahead! I'm winning the race, what an odd sensation. I inhale the idea over and over until it's unreal. Am winning a race, what race? And what am I winning? Things may change tomorrow—a fall, some broken bones, lost maps, a lost pony, lostness. Lost direction, a lost mind, tomorrow, tomorrow— tossed in lostness. I'm too weak to tighten the reins on my mind. I haven't forgotten certain ideas about ways out—dropping from the race and into fiction, riding horses all the way to my heart, or to an ocean near Japan. Bernard Moitessier didn't care to sail up to the finish line when he was on the brink of winning the 1968–1969 circumnavigatory race—instead he just carried on around two-thirds of the globe, finally pulling up in the South Pacific when it felt right.

I turn my head on its side and feel dreams trickling into my ears. By morning I'll forget how soft and sweet the scenes are— circles of sound tongued around me, miniature pianos all afly.

XXXII

On midwinter mornings Mum sometimes chucked cups of water on me to end my hibernation. I needed schooling. Children need schooling. We think of them just as we think of animals. Except I think of animals as gods. Stand beside the shoulder of a horse, and evaporate.

In high school, brains were the aim of the game. We learned to store up facts like noble larders. By the time we left, we'd been taught many expensive ideas, but I lacked any desire to use them. Where next? Oxford, of course. In my household, this word summoned our lust—your life threatened to pass its sell-by date if you didn't get into Oxford University, which I did not, and you weren't meant to come to Mongolia for a horse race instead. Thinking was supreme, and intelligence orgasmic.

Animals do not "think," in the abstract sense. Ask the European philosophers. Over the centuries, they have cast the pause between animals and humans as a division. Animals "lack" in comparison to humans. Animals are not moral. They do not have will. They are not political. They do not have nations. Heidegger calls animal existence "poverty." Hegel insists that "the courage of an animal or a robber . . . are not its true forms." And Adorno says "the eyes of animals . . . seem to mourn that they are not human." On they go, fingering their stale beards.

Behind the centuries lies the animals' silence. I think we might be envious of how they are complete in their bodies. That a donkey's sensory system is more highly developed than any philosopher's is my favorite fact. In the seconds I cease pretending—aboard a horse, up against a tree—I remember body before all else.

Unzip my skin and you might find luminescent blue rubber ready for a swim. I am not really human. And nor, am I sure, is anyone else.

Girl. People are not sure, on any given day, where you will begin. I can tell that you yourself wish you knew. What you are. Whether you have a core at all. Or are simply layers of air.

On the sixth day of the race I wake with a terrified start, as if Mum's water has just splashed across my patiently closed eyes. In the last parts of the night I slipped in and out of love, old loves stale but still golden, raised from the past in dreams. A glimpse of March, summer rising. On dead grass I stand with a boy-man clutching my wrists. We all spill into one another and thrive. Every person I meet is lit by my impressions of those I used to know. Yes, we are pouring into each other, as time pours into itself.

✦

A stack of blankets lies across my shoulders. I push them off and leap into the dawn. This is the penguin, dropping from her iceberg. I move fast to keep warm. The long-gone loves retire to their caverns, coaxed home by the coldness.

Staff in Ulaanbaatar chain-smoked through the night as they tracked the vets racing to monitor both the main pack and the front runners. On her satellite phone at 2 a.m., Helen, the South African vet, reported to Ulaanbaatar after four hours of rest. How was she functioning on so little sleep? asked the organizers in Ulaanbaatar. *I had a bath in the stream*, she replied.

Competitors are tumbling home. Twenty-one now remain in the race. Thanks to the speed of The Lion and the gray horse before him, I have broken a Derby record. Four and a half horse stations covered in one day. I have about seven legs left, which could mean two whole days—a long time.

A paler shade of eaten green surrounds the pony's iron rod. I untie the rope and let him nuzzle my face briefly. He stalks over to the horse line with his body slanting and his eyes alive. The walk of a horse has the same four-beat footfall pattern as the gallop. They can bolt from a standstill. So you never feel quite certain, a trick awaiting you at each corner.

I know he'll be difficult to tack up after yesterday's bucking fit. Twitchy horses are in league with the spirit world, according to one northern and eastern European myth. The halter needs to come off; the bridle needs to go on. Between these steps he will be in limbo, free for whichever breed of freedom he's plotting.

I drift around him, trying to tune into his brain. He is smiling so sublimely.

Are you in heaven? I ask.

I tell you, he is smiling out the back end of the century.

Halter off. Bridle approaching. He lunges back. Two steps and he shoots out of my grasp. I scramble for mane but miss. He is trotting away up the hill and as he gets smaller I get calmer, thinking the air will only be quiet when I board the plane home. Until then, there's a delight in the not-knowing, in these whatever-next sort of seconds.

The more I trot after him, the more certain he is to move away. I pull up my socks and retreat. What shall I ride today? All the goats come running in. I laugh and take my laughter back in through my ears. This sort of moment is my favorite of all the lonely ones.

Inside the ger the boy with long legs is dreaming on the floor. I tap him and gesture for help. Relaxed as ever, he moves slowly to dress while I wait outside, where the wind swings the canvas at the brim of the ger. When he emerges he moves his gaze to the distant pony and goes up the shrubby incline loosely, as if the earth is walking him.

I follow behind. He nears the pony and whistles three long notes. The dun does not move. He's so close I'm sure the pony will flee in fright. All is held still by a rope between their minds, one I can barely touch. He links his gangly arms around the pony's neck. I witness their standing embrace from afar. This is beautiful. Time for me to leave, I think.

After we've led the pony back down the hill, I suggest to the boy, whose name I'll never know, that he mount before I do. *No way*, he seems to say, amazed, and when I ask again, his head chases the question away and the dimples in his cheeks deepen. So he holds the reins while I get on. The pony bucks slightly, then we are *choo choo* and gone. I wave goodbye to the clarity of the dawn, his peace, that comfort, unhinged from the race.

Trotting up the hill pass, we see birds flit through fleecy pines.

The horse is talking, the earth is whispering, the grass is humming, and who knows what sounds they hear from me. The pine branches, bent sideways by wind, suggest I shut my eyes. *Shut your eyes and you shall see better.*

Are you sad? You look so sad, I tell the trees.

We only look sad because you can't imagine a stillness that's not.

I would cease here and holler at the wrinkled bark, write letters to their roots. See how ribbons blow in winters gone, and listless lives sink into song. I would. If only I didn't feel the need to keep manning the lead.

The ovoo on the peak is a high pile of branches. No time to circle. On the descent, the groan of an engine rises behind us. Richard's jeep overtakes and halts. He clambers out in a T-shirt and crouches in the dew, uttering one sentence as I pass.

"She's twenty minutes behind you." He delivers this in monotone, barely lifting his lips. The man seems no longer to ask me questions. He just serves up carefully constructed lines. I think I might christen him the Ghost of the Race—appearing and disappearing, stilling us all.

I watch his jeep descend and unfurl the land. The sea of grass dances in his wake, beckoning our arrival. As the horse trots on, I am gripped by mild terror. *She's behind you, she's behind you, nuh-nuh na nuh-nuh.* At the bottom of the hill a spirit in the shape of a dog canters up to us. Nose to the ground, he circles and pauses ahead. I look around to where he came from and see the pink dot bleeding down the hill.

Within the minute the dog disappears, snorkeling the earth on some journey north. I stop turning my head and the land funnels us left. I can't have Devan thinking I'm honoring her approach.

And I don't want to be too precise a target of her ambition. She barely knows who I am—she refers to me as "Laura" and is under the illusion that she's younger than me. Her eye is on the prize, and details such as these are insignificant. I don't think it will have crossed her mind that my drive is to bring her down to earth, and that in this way, she has created her rival. I want to put a stop to the prophecy she made at start camp.

Sadly my competitive parts, which I took so much trouble to suppress as a teenager, have needed to return for the purpose. Maybe this is proof that certain aspects of our characters sit in a freezer somewhere, always ready to defrost.

If I were to say to myself *I want to win and I care*, I might begin to find the whole competition less exciting. But instead, such words circle at the edge of my consciousness like giant birds too distant to be truly seen, let alone examined. I ride with a mysterious compulsion, not knowing where it comes from.

With a woman in the lead and three more on her tail, the race seems likely to have its first female winner this year. It's strange it has taken so long, considering half the entrants are usually women, and that female riders outnumber men in many countries.

They intrigue me, these mini republics of equestriennes. Do women just really love horses? Or do horses love women? There's the Freudian theory that women direct their erotic energy towards horses, whereas straight men often relate to them through dominance. But is there no love other than the erotic? One of the women in Robert Vavra's 1981 book *All Those Girls in Love with Horses* is Aunt Lucinda. The author asks her about her first horse, Be Fair, who had natural balance and a generous spirit. "I'm told that love like that only comes round once a lifetime," she remarked.

My oldest brother George has suggested I'm the one who rides because I'm a product of my gender, and that may be so, but perhaps one of us just needed to partake in the family tradition. Though my father sidelined the horses, they ran through the house in Appleshaw and you could sense this in the way my mother can smell water.

Then again, I may have needed horses more than my brothers did. Aunt Lucinda's equestrian career spanned the shift from horses as military and transport animals to horses as sports animals and pets, increasingly aligned with women—in the UK, at least. In fact, riding has offered a counterexistence to women since before the times of Lady Godiva or the Amazons of Scythia, one in which we can be demanding and assertive.

If horses can make us powerful, they can also make us feel powerless—it's the persuasion required to access their power that I find compelling.

Maybe the approaching pink dot isn't Devan. Maybe it's a floating pom-pom. Some Hello Kitty debris? Cinderella on the fly? My horse is tired, the urtuu is near, we cannot move faster. When the hill steepens, we slow to a walk and a rustling sweeps in. Devan's chest pushes at the wind as she rises and plunges to the rhythm of her pony's trot.

"Good morning!" she sings, cheerfully.

The spoken words surprise the grassland and surprise me too. Devan makes no eye contact and I'm wary of her tone. Like last night, I am too incensed by her to reply. Is this half rude or fully rude?

Who's worse, Devan or Lara?

I like to think my silence might disarm her. I don't want to play a part in the story she's set on. Though I do so love to follow it, one step behind.

Her rain jacket crinkles and her blond hair blooms as she sails on. Like a waterfall she drops off the landscape ahead.

Devan has taken her lead back.

Oh well.

Oh hell.

XXXIII

The urtuu, number 18 of 25, is plotted in this basin but I can't see it. Has the family packed up and moved to another valley since the organizers came through two months ago? We zigzag down the hill, praying that tumbledown goat shack over there has forty ponies tied behind it . . . but no, on we go, looping round a jutting hillock. Ah, the station is here in the next chapter, bedded on the turf by a lazy river.

Richard is languishing next to his jeep. Devan grazes her pony, waiting for its rate to slow. Maybe they've just had a conversation and have nothing left to say.

I enter into discussion with a man who raises his dark eyebrows to explain his fastest horse is being watered down at the river—if only I wouldn't mind waiting a little for my nineteenth pony. Devan eyes us from behind. She has already picked her next horse and did not ask anyone from the Daariijav family for advice.

When someone returns from the water with a string of horses, the herder points out the leftmost horse for me.

Devan strides around and aims her arm at it. "I think I'll take that one."

I gesture to speak, but all I produce is a swimming "ummm." I have an urge to slap her with a fish. Does she not startle herself?

The interpreter jumps to my assistance. "No, that horse is for Lara."

Devan shifts her eyes as though to look at me, but her beam skips on by.

Behind us, Richard grins and casts a line. "Now, now. Don't get competitive, you two."

Dear Devan, with all her thick blond hair and chest-led rises to the trot. Do I just find her so extreme because I only spend five-minute periods with her? Perhaps I've been constructing an elaborate muckheap out of nothing. Not for a moment have I tried to access her inner world: no idea if she hates me back, what she fantasizes about apart from winning, or whether she still has a relationship with her childhood teddy bear.

I used to love winning just as much as she does, but it was accompanied by shame. As a nine-year-old in the swimming pool, facing down, my expressed effort was hidden. Running races in the London parks, I never wanted to commit the crime of appearing fast, so I strode with my arms hung like insouciant curtain tassels and trailed my legs on the long stretches. I was irritated by the girl in my class who stuck her bottom out and told everyone her personal bests for a lap of breaststroke. It was as though she canceled out all my efforts at shrugging off the world.

Somewhere along the line I seem to have learned that overt ambition is distasteful. The glimpse I've had of Devan so perfectly bulldozes any of those ideas about modesty, I might just be jealous of her. A certain vet admires Devan for being "who she is," "pretense-free." Of course, politeness isn't what we're here for, is it?

I don't know where my love of shrugging comes from. I'm just suspicious of demonstrations of supreme willfulness. They make me think of villainy. It's the demonstration as much as the willfulness itself that I mistrust. Why intentionally alienate other people? Maybe I just want to see Devan fallible.

She lays her tack on a herder's outstretched arms and steps back with her hands on her hips. I watch her watching him saddle her pony, then I turn for the ger. Richard needs shots of me with food for the website. Gleefully I glug down some white tea, unsure whether my scruffy appearance is going to ruin or enhance the photo. Perhaps my hair will require an operation when I get back. It's so dirty even the grease has taken flight, and the curls at my ear lobes have gone solid.

Richard is quiet, minding himself and the angle of his camera. I'm unaware his photos have already been transmitted off the steppe. They can see me at home. This should dispel any rumors about me wandering alone in the wilderness—clearly there's a photographer giving me some occasional company, not to mention Devan—but it turns out people imagine what they like, and in this case I think they want me lonesome with the land. I don't know why.

When I finally see Richard's photos, my memory separates the photographed ponies from the unphotographed. The fifteen he never sees through his lens remain with me, but for the snapped ten, I lose something. The photos place me outside of them.

✦

We have to rise, my legs and I. Through the door I see a horse figure dashing away from the urtuu. It's the pink dot larger than ever, her heels dipped low for the charge. I leap outside into the vision of a gray-blue bird and run to the pony, who fires us out of the station. We are in motion and changing.

Wink, and we're gone.

XXXIV

Devan's ahead. This is a bit of a relief. I found it torturous always having to look for her behind me. Chasing feels more positive. Up the Khanui River valley we fly, locked in a cantering lullaby as the winds of time rush by. This is a horse sensitive and lightfooted. He hears engine noise, he bolts. I sense Richard behind but I'm wrong. It's the ABC monster advancing, and with the tree shelter behind us there's nowhere to hide.

The motoring red van draws up to our side and Alex's head squirms out of the window as the horse throttles along, almost out of hand. His camera is perched in his hands, poised to drink pixelated color out of me.

"Lara!"

More questions, many, many questions as he takes shots of the horse. There's so much space surrounding us we can't look much like action. When Alex hurls his final question, the horse is out of rhythm, zipping along at a gallop I can't allow.

"We're gonna go catch Devan now. Any messages for her?"

I pause, censoring six sentences a second. "Send her a kiss." I shout it. They swerve away up the valley towards the strengthening sun. I no longer chuckle after these encounters. I don't like their words. I feel like their pet, their postcard. Why not let it all be forgotten?

And wow, how I go at it now.

I am racing for the finish and racing for something else, a thing that changes with the wind, a thing I may never know nor think nor really see, only circle around, like a startled horse inspecting a coiled snake.

We move fast. I can't spot Devan in the textures ahead. Behind the hills are miniature rivers tickling one big river. We wriggle across tributaries, fall through bogs, the thickening air, the smell of sage, the sweat lathered white against his black-coated shoulders. Beyond the waterlands a blue sky widens. I check my GPS. *Follow me*, the arrow commands, and I do because in the sunlight I can't see the screen's more subtle shading, which illustrates hills. *You twit*, the eTrex will later say, *for believing my arrow*.

We trot across the flats for 5 kilometers. The pony stops often to drink. This is the oven of the midday steppe. I hear the heat oozing out of the day. At the end of the plain, he ceases to be his lightning self. The hill ahead is much higher than it appeared from the river—more like a mountain, in fact. How it fooled me. How most things fool me.

I wince for the weary being beneath me. He scrambles us up the slope of dread, trying his best. Sweat crawls farther into my eyebrows. We see mountains at the top, so many mountains. I want to scream them into flatness. I'm a devout follower of tracks—I am, I am—but the tracks head right and the station is left, beyond a set of reckless young cliffs.

Chomp. I bite the air. I let us go down, he stumbles, so we go up, and it's too vertical. We stop, it's too angular. The slates below loosen. Any second I imagine being poked off the mountainside with the flick of some god's finger. I think back to the start-camp pony who marooned himself up a hillock. This is steeper, the pony braver, the air far hotter, and the whole situation very much more serious since I am serious now, serious about winning, in all seriousness.

A sight drops into my frantic thoughts: pink dot, moving on the slow course of a star. The red van is pursuing her. They're on their way to urtuu 20 already.

I was angsty that day, after the early-morning calm. If I'd spent the past days trying to get inside the tunnel of the race, on this day— the sixth—I seemed to have spouted out the other end. My sense of my surroundings weakened and I was barely present, even as the horse stared out from his nose muttering, *There is no world but this.* I wish I'd known some technique for staying there. Not "there" in a particular spot, but there in my body in those moments, the ones that kept leaping along. Moving and yet not.

I was facing a pointlessness the race had, until then, mainly submerged. Things hurt—body, mind—and I wondered if it was simply life. I look back at this nineteen-year-old and think she is probably just plain sad, but the word is unknown.

And the horse carried her, and the horse carried her. All day long, the horses carried her. As she rode down the drop, motoring for the next set of mini-cliffs below, she was trapped in a cycle of heavy thoughts, as incessant as the rocks setting slide after slide in motion below her. Could she joke with this black dog, tease it out of herself? She comes to a woeful conclusion: she can ride the horses, but she cannot ride her mind.

I'm sure it makes things easier not having any human company. Rhythms move inside me to build me back up. Soon I'll be cantering away from the mountainside with enough speed to quell the worst of my thoughts.

The valley floor is soothing as a bath after a long day.

We reach the station, where you can smell the nearby river. Baska's interpreter walks up to me as I ride in. I'm told, in a tone of some authoritative pleasure, that Devan is an hour ahead and I must sit a fifty-six-minute penalty at the next urtuu because I apparently "rode until 8:58 p.m. last night."

I jump out of my ears. I only rode until 8:33 p.m. How can I prove the error when I was alone and spent the night with a family unconnected to the race?

I file an impassioned complaint with Tsetsgee while Baska takes the heart rate. His head is slanted away from the race. He doesn't seem to care. But then there's that thing about people who flop their arms and appear not to care—sometimes they care more than anyone, care enough they don't want anyone to know they care, because the caring might lose force if it reveals itself.

✦

I run to the ger, where strings of drying blocks of milk line the eaves—carefully cut shapes of yak's milk, cow's milk, mare's milk, sheep's milk. I tried one of these blocks yesterday; it was an effort to conceal my repulsion. Social disaster number 76.

Without time for a meal, I stuff my pockets with *boortsog*, the morning and midday pastries deep-fried in mutton fat. They're so hardy you could send them round the world in the post. I haven't seen many vegetables lately. I treasured the streaks of carrot in the sushi yesterday afternoon.

I ferry boortsogs down my throat as I pace over to the horse. Without Charles at the station, the race feels like a dull rush again. Part of me is disappointed by the way I move through the urtuu so automatically. I glimpse the river, where the grass is eaten down to velvet, and envisage a holiday on its bank. *What am I doing?* I begin to ask myself, seeing Baska eyeing me bound up to the saddle. I long for a time of no-asking.

"Don't think, feel," says Aunt Lucinda to cross-country riders. She finds brain surgeons particularly difficult to teach because they so love to think everything through. "As soon as you think, you move too soon."

I *choo choo* the twentieth horse away from his home but he struggles so much I return him to the station, where everyone has shrunk back into their routines. They swivel heads and shoulders to receive me again. I thrust the tack onto another, younger pony, itching to get on, but this one is just as reluctant. He wiggles in an odd, untrained gait along a sorry highway of mud tracks while I chew on boortsog, taunted by the impending penalty. Our afternoon shadow bumps along beneath us. Somewhere a herd of wistful mares canters by, foals clinging to their sides, creatures little and wild. The reluctant pony neighs and veers towards their glimmering coats. We push on, into the void.

XXXV

It's about quarter past three when the reluctant pony delivers me into urtuu twenty. Each of the last few stations has seemed full of bodies, but this one's a party. I stare with astronaut eyes. Charles winds his way to the front of the crowd to greet me, and it's in these seconds before we say anything that the magnetism of his static is most irresistible.

"Headquarters," he announces, "have got the penalty wrong. The satellite trackers can be inaccurate."

You don't say, I think, sliding off. Instead of the original fifty-six-minute proposal, they make me sit a sixteen-minute penalty, convinced I rode until 8:38 p.m.

The station, surrounded by worn-down earth, seems like it has been here for a while. The horse lines tip over the hillside into a steep brown bowl and the smell of wet dust is mystifying.

A young girl, maybe nine years old, edges in to fill up my water bottle while Charles tells me Clare has hit the ground from a bucker. Apparently she's now riding without her kit, clinging to third place with Kirsten after leaving Chloe behind to recover from her sickness.

Neither Charles nor I knows at this point that Devan's father has been tweeting to the Mongol Derby page, asking if I've sat my penalties and complimenting his daughter's progress. Not that my father would have been doing differently, if he knew how to work Twitter.

When the girl returns with my bottle full, she looks at me keenly, with a warm, precise smile. It's enough to draw apart the curtains in my chest, and the moment fixes itself in my heart. Charles's presence dilutes it, but this I do not mind.

The next leg has been passing with all the monotony of a sea crossing when, an hour and a half in, the pony lies down beneath me in the manner of a devoted fireside rug. I find myself with both feet on the ground.

What are you doing? I ask him. I have never known a horse to take a seat.

Joining you, he replies.

Charles wanted me to choose a spotty, dog-like creature for the leg instead of this horse, and I now regret not listening to him. Amid the indecision, Charles had stopped to look at me without blinking, which caused my stomach to jump into my throat, where it has been perching all afternoon, lizard-like.

It really hits me during this leg that love—some form of it—brings me alive and strings me along. Always has, always will—even and especially the unrequited and the unhappened love, the Case Pendings in the Department of Romance.

From what I can tell—well, I'm only nineteen—love affairs in the England I grew up in aren't obvious. People tend not to display the full extent of their feelings, letting love quietly hold them together behind the scenes, even in January, even in queues. The problem, if it is a problem at all, is that I rarely get to the affair. I just wait like a bird feeder. I haven't really clocked my lack of boldness in love, let alone taken action to reverse it.

The day lightens when I work out there can't be more than 200 kilometers to the finish, which means I may finish the race tomorrow evening. Nearing urtuu 21, we reach a soum called Ulziit, which is ruled by offensive clouds. A chill enters me. The town is frontier-like. It summons a full stop out of the infinite steppe.

We arrive at a torrential river on Ulziit's far side. Her banks look overwhelmed. So many of the rivers I've passed are roaring—I think it must be the time of year. Summer has reached capacity.

Rain starts pecking my cheeks—a series of micro-prods: *go-go-go*. At the river the horse enlarges his nostrils into black holes, snorting air at the torrent. He quicksteps back to assess, from which position he spends several minutes ignoring my urging hips and my heel pokes at his rib cage. He also ignores my comments about how the bridge will be a solid thing, separate from the water, very traversable.

It just so happens that the good old fishcakes from ABC catch up with us now. The driver, a blond, beer-bellied American, opens his door to tell me I should dismount and lead my horse. I wish I'd thought of this myself. The pony's eyes drop to watch my feet walk on just ahead, suggesting to him the ground is safe. Come now, come now, it's alright, I say, trying to turn myself into a site of conviction, a leader. Over we jitter, reaching a wall of cloud.

✦

I walk the last kilometer of the twenty-first leg on foot, feeling stacks of earth beneath me, studying the tendrils of land beyond the coming camp, readying myself to ride out into night again—the pony at the end of my reins already dropping into the past. There's still an hour and a half until cutoff. But when I reach Charles in the gray light of urtuu 21, he announces the race has been "held," whatever that means—it isn't a term they mentioned at the briefing or in the rule book.

Charles's nonchalant tone dismantles my momentum. He explains that Devan and I have ridden too fast for the vets and stewards to keep up. We need to wait until morning to continue. Devan will leave at 7 a.m. while I'll wait until 8:25 to maintain the hour-and-twenty-five-minute gap between us. I have lost so much to her today. She is currently fast asleep in the corner of a ger, breathing dreams of victory.

I remember hearing a rider declare, during a meal of bright-pink-pasted sandwiches at start camp, that this was "base camp," as though we were about to ascend Everest. Winning the race was "the equivalent of climbing Everest without an oxygen tank," added another. No one really believed them, but I like thinking of two people hanging from a mountain cliff. They can't afford to quarrel, even if they hate each other.

Ahimsa, a concept Gandhi emphasized, involves concentrating on not hating your enemy. I can't say ahimsa is on my mind this evening, with the finish line so close (maybe I'm too juvenile to indulge in ethical practice). But later I will question whether my obsession with Devan qualifies as a skewed kind of love. Albertus Magnus of the 1200s, a German Catholic friar and bishop who was later made a saint, saw great power in the intensity of any emotion. "A certain power to alter things indwells in the human soul, . . . particularly when she is swept into a great excess of love or hate or the like. . . . Everyone can influence everything magically if he falls into great excess."

I feel there's no chance of my winning from this far behind. Might it be time to skip my way out of here? With only four stations to go until the end, I feel freedom approaching—oh, the very idea—a mass of fatigue falls out of my body. I spot the lake and want a naked swim through its water. Off I go, bounding down the herby, stony ground in a towel, merry me merry me merry me. I do not feel the pain in my bare feet. Mongolia is one of the highest countries in the world, with an average elevation of around 1,500 meters, and I can't actually breathe that well when I run. This might be why I've sometimes had the sense that I'm on the moon out here.

Charles has seen me disappear and reported to headquarters that I've gone for a dip. "It is a bit cold for a swim," he tells them. I grind to a halt at a muddy marsh ruled by flies, where I commence the swim in the spirit in which I set out, and emerge dirtier. Miserable lake. Fishless.

Up at the cars below camp, I find Charles, Richard, and a few others talking. I'm too far away to interrupt and too sheepish to go nearer, but Charles screams as I pass.

"Watch out!"

A sinister giant lizard—was it a chameleon, I later wonder?—is poised beneath me. About to strike. I whinny in terror, leaping away into Richard's camera, my towel almost falling. Quickly I replace my panic with intense interest—I've been wanting to meet more steppe wildlife. We stand in a circle around the stunned beast. Charles crouches to examine it. Maybe an upbringing in South Africa has left him expert on such creatures.

"Highly poisonous," he says. "I'll catch it."

If there's one way to prove your worth, it is to launch yourself onto a poisonous lizard five hours from the nearest hospital. I clench my jaw as Charles lunges with a towel and lands on it. He stands up clutching the toweled creature against his chest. It may now bite him.

Someone bursts into laughter. It is fake, fake they say, tipping the lizard out of the towel. It's made of plastic. This has to be one of the larger letdowns of my life so far. On par with the evening I thought I was eating hawk, when really I had misheard the word "pork."

ABC Alex follows me back to my bed. He wants to video me unpacking. I have to ask myself what he's really after, since such a clip can hardly make compelling television. I've been monosyllabic with him all day.

His crew car was nigh on stapled to my back for that last leg on the reluctant pony, and nothing would shake it off. Each time I'd said "Ho" to walk, they drove up to our side and drained all our peace. Alex's window would glide down, revealing his white T-shirt, his black combed hair, and his inappropriate smile.

"We're on Team Lara!" he shouted during one of these episodes. I suppose he wanted to flatter me into a few more comments for his documentary. Already he had drawn out thoughts I'd prefer to have left unformulated.

"Devan's boring. It's more entertaining following you," he shouted.

I found it difficult to imagine how Devan—my engine, my fuel—could be classified as "boring." If it had been a dinner party I'd have thought, Oh, ah, must remain polite to this man. But it wasn't a dinner party, and I didn't reply.

Now that I'm off the horse, I politely display my bungee ropes, my sun creams, and my bag full of six types of no-longer-identifiable pills, from which I am now taking regular doses.

Jeeps and camper vans are drawing in, positioning themselves for tomorrow. With any luck it will be my final day, though there are racers farther back who will ride another three days before nearing the finish. As crew members gather, my ecstasy grows, and I revel in the use of toilet paper once more. No one takes any notice as I dip in and out of the party, bluebottle thing. I have the soothing feeling that although they're ignoring me, they're present at this camp because of me (and Devan), positioned to launch into a full day of monitoring me (and Devan).

At the edge of camp I hurdle Richard's one-man tent a few times, not once cleanly. Brother Arthur has a better technique, and always beats me at such feats. There was a joke before I left home about how I'm always second to him. I think of this now and it feels very sore, with only a slither of funny.

In the end I don't eat dinner. I've no appetite; in fact, I feel sick as I stagger into the darkened ger for bed. I bump the metal bed legs. Ouch, pulsing shins. I only notice illness has taken me when I fail to contemplate Devan. She's just a couple of meters away but long since departed for the realm of sleep. I'm not surprised I'm ill, since so many other riders have been unwell. I presume I'm suffering the same sickness.

I lie down and think about whether I'll be too ill to ride tomorrow. I know we all spend periods of our lives unwell in some way, but I think my body decides the timing—I believe in illness, I believe in accident, though I can't decide in what way. Is it time to give up? I could sleep for forty-eight hours and still ride through the finish in good time. Somehow fourteenth position sounds attractively inconsequential.

By midnight, the party outside seems to have devolved into a few slow conversations. I really need to throw up. Two members of the race staff are kissing on the far floor of the ger as vomit enters my mouth. I haul off the creaky bed, noisier than an old trampoline, and land on the person beneath me. Tsetsgee? She squirms in her spongy sleep and resumes unconsciousness. Swallowing my sick I dash outside, where night has gulped up the day. I collapse behind the ger. Headlamps swivel in my direction.

"Oi, Charles, who's squatting over there?"

There is muffled laughter.

I circle the camp in search of barrels of water, nearly splatting onto Richard's one-man tent in the process. Undetectable window panes must be a nightmare for flies.

When the barrels emerge from the murk, I prepare to wait half an hour for the distillation tablets to fight the Battle of the Bacteria. But I'm too thirsty. Five minutes in, water is pouring down my throat like a herd of heroic stallions, freeing the parched plains of my body. The vets are snoring now, and I am the lonely daughter of an evening gone cold.

✦

This brother of mine Arthur, he's got a wispy fringe, backward-leaning posture, short trousers, and well-placed moles. Somewhere around the age of ten, he forgot how to smile for photographs—I think because he was embarrassed by his teeth.

"I'm not sure she really understands about life yet," he once said of me. Our relations are cordial, if slightly cold—certainly never affectionate. I did once accidentally cut off three of his fingers. He fell over just in front of me and the side of my ski went through his hand. The SOS team took him away and I was left looking back up at a trail of blood on the white mountainside.

In a week's time I will read a message from him, sent through tonight. "*The whole world is watching (I am not joking)—everybody following your every move. I LOVE YOU.*"

XXXVI

Seven is my lucky number. It's Aunt Lucinda's lucky number too. I'm sure I didn't copy her—lots of people like seven. It crouches between rounded, even numbers with all the energy of an odd underdog.

Horses make me superstitious. In eventing, riders are identified with two- or three-digit numbers when they ride cross-country. If my competition number doesn't add up to seven, I am worried for the day. It's not as literal as "Seven will protect me from rotational falls," it's more the sense that it will regulate and enforce the future through a chaotic code I can't quite see.

As the night passes I find myself thinking of seven. Tomorrow will be the seventh day of riding. Something might happen. This thought glances through my mind and returns to pass more slowly. Then I think of the obvious numbers: the urtuus. Four legs remain, meaning three urtuus beyond this one—22, 23, 24. No sevens there. If the finish line were an urtuu, it would be the 25th, and the digits

2 and 5 do make 7. But it's not an urtuu; it's the finish line. Nothing can happen after the finish, so I flick to a conclusion: I won't be overtaking Devan tomorrow. I do not know this completely, but I suspect knowingly, feel I understand the outcome deeply.

Beyond my number jumbling, I have one solemn thought: If Devan triumphs, the world will have gone ever so slightly wrong.

I agree it's a little too much, but it is a thought that flits by.

The seventh day begins in the sog of an unwell sleep. I swim up to the surface, luring my dreams out a back of my brain. All night long they teased me, tickling my predicaments to life. Horses careen down a back drive in one dream (*escape! escape!*), and somewhere there was a vision of my father hot and my mother cold, both howling preverbally, no alphabet in their brains, just one large moon of pain. It's too soon to dissect that one. There were also goats flying all night, nearly dying, and tongues turning corners. Fish singing riptide hymns, while heavens opened and resealed for quieter times—plain bodies and the hairs upon them, nothing more.

Nothing more. The light extinguishes dreams. A rat gallops across the floor and I'm vertical, stroking my tiny tummy with the satisfaction of an evil marmot. I've been up all night waiting to vomit. I have not eaten and I cannot eat. There is nothing left of me but me. I'll have to draw energy from my head and the horses. Take the tiredest of dogs for a run, and watch her give every muscle she never knew she owned to the sprint.

My old friend Miranda, who has immense social stamina but doesn't care about sport, flings messages into my unmanned inbox. *"This is the most exciting sport I've ever watched,"* and hours later, *"I*

can't go to sleep I keep refreshing the map qnwojdljakakfhdakdans."
They have all resorted to the dramatic. Me? I'm almost too sick to
care.

what early rising train is this?
To where does it intend to escape from this sleepy life?

These lines by Ayurzana Gun-Aajav, a contemporary Mongolian
poet, make me question my urge to escape. I push into morning,
resisting my desire to ride out through the back door of the race, on
a journey away, perhaps towards home—which is where? We never
quite decide, so heading home, we go nowhere. Maybe home is just
all that we leave behind.

For the first time in the race it seems I've slept through my alarm. I
must be truly ill. Devan has left. There aren't many minutes before
my 8:25 departure time. I fling bits of equipment out of the ger,
where they sit, petrified. On this day, I will do things without love.
The thick air drenches me. My body sweats a strange sweat. A line
of ants starts crawling up my calf, as if to fetch me for a party below.
Take me, gently, lower my body down.

Richard hovers nearby, tracking my packing with his camera.
"I'm going to collapse," I tell him. The stomach bug has me. His
mouth moves below the camera, saying something about the other
competitors who had food poisoning.

"It only tends to last fifteen hours or so," he says, his feather-
light Irish accent caressing me. "You should be better by midday."

He's speaking so softly I'm surprised I can hear.

✦

In the corner of my eye Charles drives out of camp, heading west for the riders behind us. The window pane between us lets me look him in the eye. Do I dare venture further than these looks? I turn my core to face his car as it passes the last ger, and he waves. There's no knowing when I might see him again. His engine sound dies into an elsewhere.

I lumber down to the horse line like a giraffe on the moon, but find myself in need of the toilet again when I get there.

Maggie laughs. "How are you going to stay on a horse for four hours?"

I don't know. *Don't get ahead of the movement.* We must be stronger than we imagine, must somewhere be carrying a force, stuffed into our chests, probably blackberry-shaped.

Up at the toilet, I squat and feel my headache prick. I look out at the morning earth, still spread with dew, and the low-leaning sky. There are 160 kilometers between here and the finish. Four legs—twelve hours. Every morning I've studied the map book and ensured my route. Today no no, too ill, too turtlish. Tucked inside my wrinkles. I'm an ancient in the race's lifespan.

An hour and twenty minutes ago, Devan rode out on the fastest pony at the station. I'm lifting my foot to the stirrup of a lifeless gray when the ABC crew pincers me.

"Any last wishes, Lara?"

"For Devan to fall down a marmot hole."

Oh dear. Sickness has made me transparent. Time to rattle my way out of here. I heave up onto the gray.

He makes no movement. How can he be the second-fastest horse at the—

He snaps my question in half. Brings his hooves alive. I hear the sound of our sound catching up with us. We are ripping through the plain, his ears flat back like a hare's. Cloud surrounds and makes the world feel small. Three hundred meters out, Richard takes a photo of my eyes falling out of my head—exhaustion, delight, I look like a hooligan. He gives this shot to the BBC.

All leg, I barely move my body. It seems you can guide a horse by thought alone, thisaway, thataway, bending through the scrubland.

Alex's red van hangs about, but I'm mute. No more blossoming laughter. He's left with the streak of ice at my center.

When we come to a road crossing that the map book describes as "quite busy," part of me feels let down by the fact there isn't a vehicle in sight. Today I wanted car eyes glancing into me, pictured them questioning their direction as I rode horizontally across them. People from home with blurred faces.

I don't think the Prior-Palmer family, if they are watching, will realize I am ill and cannot win. It is late evening for them, and I am just a dot on their map, smaller than a star in the faint English sky. I hear a sibling-like subconscious musing—what is this bolt, wherefrom this blue? Girl looks to be functioning. Out there, on the steppe. History acting upon her.

Am I illuminated by the distance?

Urtuu 22 sits behind a square-topped mountain that might turn into a castle later in geological time. I cleave to its side until the urtuu comes into view. I love the first sighting of my temporary home. The pony canters me all the way in, spooling out over the flatlands, pinned to a nine-mile moon. I must have underridden him.

Can I convey the warmth I feel, sealed and barely mentionable, as his hooves pull up to pause his charge? I step off onto soft summer mud where the boots have been pacing. His heart rate is immediately low.

"How long ago did Devan ride through?" I ask.

"About fifty minutes before you," says Erdenmunkh, through his interpreter.

On a pony the herder said would be slower than Devan's, we have somehow made up thirty-five minutes in one leg.

ABC Alex is at the station, poking his camera around, nosier than hamsters. I walk away from him, saying with newfound animal defiance, "Don't you dare follow me again." It feels wrong that he can tape me into infinity when I'm at my most finite.

For the third-last leg of the race, I was paired with a black horse who pinged me off before I took root on his back. Erdenmunkh held him while I wiped the dust from my knees and prepared to mount again. It was a buck serious enough that, when he tried to do it a second time, I had to let the reins go to divert him into a bolt. He dived out of the station and we catapulted across the plain, his legs plummeting and lifting off, blather, gallop, we went in one blink. I held myself tight and thrust my heels down in an attempt to stay with him.

A kilometer or so out of the station, his foreleg dropped into a hidden marmot hole. We spun through the air like crumpets journeying out of a toaster. I felt myself flying down to earth, where dirt and stones scraped my face and a weight rolled over me. Then my arm hauled upwards. The pony was standing, wanting to run, but my grip had caught him—somehow, through the fall, his reins had stayed looped over my fingers.

I scrambled to a crouching position while he leaned away from me with a tilted head and rolled-back eyes. Woah, friend, woah. Anything broken? I held still. Told myself to calm. Breathe. Daft to want to beat Devan, anyway. Daft to push so hard.

Stalemate. Marmots got on with their day below ground, stroking their tummies, hugging each other with glee.

Whenever I fall I'm forced to realize that my actions are shaped by whatever I think of as dignity, whether I like to display this intention or not. That dignity disappears in falling. I have no control. Maybe, if there is some bodily code, my truth comes out in this vortex moment of vulnerability.

In the aftermath of the fall, I start to question space. Why did space do that. Is space cross with me? I am cross with space. It has flipped me over and contorted me so. It had been giving me so much ordinary motion that I'd numbed myself to the possibility that anything out of the ordinary could happen. Now, splatted, I remove all expectation.

I am peeved, meanwhile, that I told ABC Alex to pop off because it means he hasn't filmed the fall. Though falls happen too quickly for me to grasp the idea that my life is in danger, they look sensationally dangerous to spectators. Alex has actually spied the accident through his binoculars and told the vet, who is reporting back to headquarters in Ulaanbaatar, who in turn will send a paramedic in my direction. They announce as much on Twitter.

After a slow self-X-ray I sense I'm not hurt, but it takes multiple attempts to get back on the panicked pony. My leg isn't rotated over him when, on the sixth attempt, he torpedoes forth as though the horizon is leaving without him, galloping over the holes with just the same blindness he offered before our fall. It seems our burial has been a mere boost for the morning.

As the hours pile higher, I begin to feel less ill. The black horse settles into our little life together, his muscles contracting back and forth in a strong trot, the beat of his feet an equine metronome. As I rise and fall, I hear the regular sounds of things out of place— saddle flaps, keyring chain—and feel the hairs at the sides of my face, enjoying our path. I tell myself about the rain I love—the drops that land on my back like the pats of a benevolent grandparent— the rain that comes to massage the air and give the land a bath, lathering it in water sweet and replete.

There's no rain today. The rainmaking magic's away. Bare blue sky holds the stage. This is a land far away from the sea; clouds sometimes struggle to make it so far. The simple sun doesn't create the right mood for the drama, though the shah of Khwarezm, Chinggis Khan's enemy, was very moved by it. He thought the sun's singularity was a sign there should only be one ruler on earth.

On we hurry under the sky into a dry river basin. We roll down bone-land. The soil seems to have risen up and subsumed whatever wanted to grow. Steamrolling around a corner, I feel my pocket lose weight. I look round to our trail and see the water bottle falling forever backwards. It has escaped from my denim vest. Likely via the same route as the map book. There must be hole construction going on somewhere but I don't want to explore. The vest only has to last a bit longer. Safe to say it has not been worth its denim aesthetic.

From the loose rocky face ahead of urtuu 23—the second-last of the race—I see the delicate shape of a horse and its rider sashaying away over the eastern hill. It is one o'clock.

I swing out of saddle suspension and land at the station, which spins like a planet.

"Was that Devan who just left?" I ask Pete the vet.

He stands with his hands on his hips, sunburnt now. "Yes. She very nearly got a penalty. Her pony's heart rate took forty minutes to come down. Five minutes from a two-hour penalty, ay."

I like the way he cares about the race so earnestly.

"Devan waited twenty minutes for the heart rate to go down at the last station, too," he adds, while taking my horse's rate, which is level after six minutes.

Prophets like Dashtseren are never expected to predict accurately. Their art lies in making a sketch of a coming possibility. Dare I risk even a sketch? I am coming to have an idea of the *meant*, as in the meant-to-be, as in the thing my mother says when birthday cakes are burnt or rain cancels the village fete. "It was meant to be."

I do not step into the ger. The race holds me taut. The tiniest person present takes my attention—a girl with pigtailed hair who clings to her mother's hip. I lack the appetite to say yes when her timid elder sister steps forward to offer me a meal, but these quiet moments in their company nudge some brightness into me.

Pete reappears, chattering on. "I asked the family where their best horse was but the one they pointed out to me has disappeared.

Come, come, let's ask again." He shuffles off as though wearing slippers. I haven't a clue that, at 48 kilometers, the next leg—the second-to-last—will be the longest of the race.

After I leave the urtuu, Pete finds out that Mr. Bayarsaikhan, who was wearing a white beret, took his best horse off the line because he thought Devan shouldn't have been made to wait for her pony's heart to go down. During Naadam—an annual Mongolian festival involving wrestling, archery, and horse racing—the fastest horse over 15 to 30 kilometers wins and heart rate plays no role. Theoretically, the horse can drop dead two strides after the finish line and still be champion. Mr. Bayarsaikhan thinks the Derby welfare precautions are unfair to the riders.

XXXVII

Maybe long-term me just likes to be alone. I am on the second-to-last leg of the race. I am on the second-to-last leg of the race. I am on the second-to-last leg of the race and I can't smile for Richard's photographs because the pressure and the ache are now too great. I'd quite like to cry.

When the dun pony and I set off, we were seventeen minutes behind Devan. But the animal beneath me canters like a camel—which is to say, he cannot canter at all. I have a share in his body for the coming hours. His bones are my bones. I leave him to his own devices and let the land around us slow down. With this, the campaign to overtake Devan ends. She stretches farther into the lead; I see this in my mind. My thought runs on as we graft up the side of a marshland river. I pray for release from the race. Voices speak to me in my head. Charles, and Richard, and home.

The ground is fertile, the grass is long, a Garden of Eden too good to ignore. Trotting through reed and bush, I forget about navigation. The GPS seems amused when I remember. We've missed the river crossing by 2 kilometers. The water's strong and I think of turning back, but there is no time (that dog that runs away, hand in hand with thought), so I let the dun's legs drop in and swim. He may not know the canter but he's fluent in doggy paddle. His head rises above the water and brings me to the other side.

We move wet thereafter, entranced by the flies hopping in the grass. *We are all going somewhere.* I believed the water when she said this. *We are pulled to our ends.* When we reach a barricade of mountains, I look around and let the land strike me. I don't know how mountains make their livings, nor do I understand the wider earth, but it does seem to have gotten here first. And when we're gone, this is what will be. Living in desertion, the land knows what I don't: no one can etch a story into earth or sky. The wind sprints the clouds away, the stage clears for another day.

Ayurzana Gun-Aajav writes:

> Today is, perhaps, my final day,
> The day to summarize for the last time
> All the things I've been thinking of for the past
>   several years.

Maybe we only ever have one day.

The leg grows long, the leg grows longer. Our route is mapped out on the GPS for this leg, but I find the trail deceiving. Ghosts of tracks peter out at every turn, confusing my instincts. We are clammy by the time the dun pony climbs the pass, where I smell slow-cooking herbs in the grass.

At the ridge we ride goodbye to the greens and peer into another vault in the earth's consciousness—rainless soil and Martian rock turrets. There's a graveyard of olive trees in the bowl. They draw up from the earth's core like detached ancestors, chuckling at the race from centuries away.

As I angle round a chalky track atop my horselegs, a creature sticks its neck out from a cave. It's ABC Alex. He grins beneath the recorder.

I do not protest his filming. "Only because it's beautiful here," I say.

Later, riders will see wild camels grazing on the other side of the basin. Perhaps they're here as I pass too. The distances escape me as I descend, seesawing along inside my head, thinking—not for the first time—of how many kilometers we might be behind Devan.

Near the final urtuu of the race, the dun pony breathes harder. He's going to keep me waiting at the station. Walking beside him with my hand on his neck, I see his eyes drip and feel bad for his wooden legs. We wind sloppily through the shade of dry trees. The grasslands are gone. The dry land mutters in pain beneath our hooves.

Can we be infinitely patient? Can we be infinitely free?

The station's white blobs rise into sight, sheltered by a link in the mountains. When I scan the land, I see a shape glide away beneath stone ridges and disappear round the corner. It is she, driving her way from the last station to the finish line aboard four dutiful legs. From this far away I could almost pick her up with a pair of tongs. How have I not fallen farther behind her on my slow pony? Was her previous horse just as slow?

A further few minutes of walking and I sign in at the final station—four gers parked below a craggy mountain cup. The sun is still high, though it's after 4 p.m. People seem hot and bothered, perhaps bored of waiting out the day. Where's Charles? How flimsy of me to wonder.

There is no English-speaking vet at the station, only Richard. He confirms Devan was the shape I saw leaving this station five minutes ago. He says she had a quick leg before but was made to wait here for thirty minutes while her pony's heart rate dropped. I don't understand why she's pushing her horses to the extent that she has to wait for them to recover.

In Haiti, Rome, and West Africa, among other places, it was once thought that you could ask your demon to spoil your enemy's luck. I wasn't thinking of that when I told ABC that I hoped Devan would fall down a marmot hole—likely *I* am the only one who has fallen down a marmot hole—but things seem to be happening. Objects contracting and expanding. Someone speaking from within the air. This future is not what it used to be. After six days of riding, Devan Horn is only minutes ahead. I'm wildly surprised.

In the Ulaanbaatar control room, organizers debate the Devan–Lara rivalry.

"In my sage-dom," writes Katy on Twitter from Ulaanbaatar, "the only thing I can think of that would cause a change in the rule book is if they get into a brawl on the finish line and one of them knocks out a) Maggie, race steward, b) my boss, race founder, or c) each other."

I don't think Devan and I in a fight would work. I'm not good at expressing anger. Can't confront others or even gather myself in the name of it.

The dun horse's heart rate is level at the first check. I move fast, barely tuning in to the atmosphere at the station. Race rules will give ponies' heart rates sixty minutes, rather than the usual 45, to level at the finish line. This rule was invented in case of a race to the line where riders cannot walk the ponies the last stretch to let them cool. Will I race Devan to the line? I fear she's just out of reach, but that can't stop me trying.

Richard is quiet now. They're all quiet. On the dirt, three boys discuss my final horse without making noise. Their caps poke at the sky. I notice the animal they throw my saddle over has legs like tree trunks, but preferring fate at this late stage, I offer no opinion. I'm at his shoulder as soon as they have tightened his girth. I lift my left foot into the stirrup and mount. I try to thread together a smile for anyone glancing at my departing face, but I have a cut on my lip and it hurts.

The final leg will take us to a place close to the site of start camp. We have traversed a wiggly loop and return now to the point of source.

XXXVIII

Squeeze calves, lift body. My last horse of the race, a dark chestnut, bucks in the canter. Devan is too close for me to go back and change horses. I tense my body against him.

For the first ten minutes Richard follows us. His head and camera sprout from the sunroof of his car. All day I've felt his photography dissolving me. I don't like performing for a future moment, not when the race is about to end.

Straight-faced, plain-toned, I shout through our wind. "Did you see him bucking? Is Devan's horse faster?"

Richard lowers his camera and squints his eyes. "'Bout the same, I should think."

At 32 kilometers, the last leg is shorter than most.

"Do you think I can canter this one all the way to the finish?" I yell.

"No, wouldn't have thought so."

He mows on ahead, sewing the plains together with his path.

Mountains line our side, from where the land runs out on an incline. The shades of hazy orange in the plain suggest, to me, a national bog park, so we stick to the tracks. The pony zigzags and throws his eyes backwards like fishing rods. As with any horse, he can see around to his tail but not directly ahead. The route to the finish is a simple straight line. He wants to go home and isn't lost enough to forget it.

By the fifth kilometer, sweat saturates his red-brown fur. On judgment day I will see Richard's photo, where my arm is raised with the goatskin whip, demanding him to keep his canter. I will question who the problem here is. Aunt Lucinda says what takes the horse forward is not speed, but desire. This boy has neither. I wriggle and rampage and gesture *Onwards!* His reply is a deep indifference.

Riding horses is only ever different each time. "That's why we continue all these years—addicted to the surprise," says Aunt Lucinda. My surprise is that I am flying a plod to the finish. In the photo he looks like liquid movement. But if you look closer, you'll notice his ears tensed back. Horses talk with their ears, and the angle is a grumpy one. No lens can see the bitterness between us.

We trudge on through the cosmic yellow plain.

such   space

Two hours in, we've only made 25 kilometers. We walk through a dip in the plain where the friendly grasses blow slowly. There is no sign of Devan ahead. With 7 kilometers to go, the race seems lost again yet it's somehow still living. I sit back and sink in to let the chestnut breathe on the lengthened rein. When I ask for canter again, he refuses. Don't look at me askance like that, my friend. Do we not have an understanding?

Choo! He bucks.

I kick, he bucks.

I stand in the stirrups and flick the rein over his neck.

He bucks with his ears pinned back.

A gang of my past selves surrounds me. In all the years of my father proclaiming advice at breakfast and the teachers issuing me with detentions, I cherished the idea that if I ever did that treacherous thing and became An Adult, I would at least know how to treat someone like myself. No force, nor any of those stupid stern teacher looks that made Mum laugh when I relayed them to her in the car. Just some understanding and togetherness.

How perfectly I forget. The harder I push, the sourer the chestnut becomes. He holds his hooves to the ground, where the grasses twitch their muscles. I get off his back and inspect him from the side. Steam is exiting his body. Too much canter? Perhaps in company he'd be going better? He might run if I lead him. I drag the reins from his mouth and sprint on the spot like a cartoon character. He moves no faster than a start-stop walk. I rest panting. Two puffy clouds reel above us, unsure which way to drift.

It seems the chestnut thinks I want the race to last forever. I lift my helmet off in abdication, ruffling my hair in relief. Have I escaped the race? A new kind of freedom visits me as the pony half closes his eyes by my dead thigh. Yet I still feel tormented. I pull my phone out from a vest pocket. I haven't turned it on since Ulaanbaatar. The welcome message is startling: *Choo choo! Train coming!*—I set it up on my flight from Beijing, before I knew "choo" meant "giddyup." I scroll down all five of my foreign contacts. Each beep sounds like a dead-end. I think I haven't thought of home, but of course it comes rushing back in the desperation. Family, so much family, an avalanche of family.

It never seems quite right to call my mother because I cannot tell what she will have in her hands, or where her other ear will be floating. But I do. I ring Appleshaw, where the ladybirds crawl and the plums have surely begun to fall, life dropping to earth in fervent portions. Mum might be gathering apples in the garden, from where she can hear the chickens waffling through morning or midday cluck, and where, too, she can spot the men of the family hovering in the windows, one shaving, one panicking at nothing, one loving his dog.

On the sixth beep, it's her. "Hello?"

"Hi, it's Lara. I don't know what to do. My horse won't move."

Silence. The chestnut dozes at my side, his nostrils looking down to earth.

"Lara? Wait. What? Lara my daughter? How are you calling me from Mongolia?"

"I don't know."

"Arthur! George! Simon! Come here! Lara's on the telephone."

Her tone is manic. It sounds like Harold isn't at home but the other two brothers are. They're far enough away to remind me this is absurd.

"Well why won't it move? Speak to Arthur."

"Kick it! Whip it!"

George shouts in the background. "Tell her to run with it!"

They are dogs jumping up. They are scarves slinging in the wind.

"He really won't move. I don't care anymore."

"No! You've got to win! She's giving up—*she's giving up.*"
Their morning sky is rising.
I say goodbye and hang up without pause.
Some lines come to mind—

> Didn't they ring you? Did no one call?
> To remind us it's a dream, wide and tall; to
> remind us it's a dream,
> and we will fall.

I head down the slope towards two gers, a pony stuffed with excuses trailing the reins, moving no faster than his start-stop walk. He's a reminder of what it is to coast at the sidelines. Of how nice it is to release myself. Of how very much *in* this race I have become. How has it all come to matter so much?

Ahead is the first encampment I've seen since the last station. I hope someone here knows what the pony is cross about. A short, blue-cloaked man sees our approach and ties his horse to the line. I bound over.

"Sain baina uu!"

He's silent. I begin my performance regardless, offering snorts and squeals to give him a sense of the pony's behavior. I also act out the bucks and do some pinned-back ears.

His reply is a smirk and a series of whispers. Maybe he has lost his voice. I listen to his words as though I'm about to divinely acquire the ability to understand Mongolian, but nothing he whispers suggests this is imminent. I'll never be convinced I've been here, in Mongolia, if I can't sit comfortably in a single phrase of the language.

A scar extending from the man's nose to his ear crinkles as he speaks. From the shapes of his pupils, I think he is drunk or high. Charles told us not to go northwest the other day because of a rowdy village en route—the antics of drunken men are chronicled by riders every year.

A mustache and a long nose make this man's face. He mimes out smoking in his tent, asking if I'd like to join. I refuse in English.

"No! I am not coming inside. There is a problem with the horse." I point back to a creature withdrawn into dreams.

I leave my helmet at his shoes and mount to display the problem. Seeing the pony buck me out of the saddle, he smiles— broken-toothed and, in places, completely toothless.

I dismount and open my arms to gesture. *Would you like to get on and feel for yourself?* He throws a hand onto my left breast and squeezes hard. As you would a lemon. When I thrust his hand away, his grin grows and he grabs my bum instead, rubbing and pinching it. I swerve out of his grasp and throw my hand through his cheek. Slap. It feels fantastic. I'm not sure I've ever slapped before.

He is staring me down with his head on an incline. His eyes are trying to focus. I feel I can outrun him in his drunken state, though it has crossed my mind that he might have a knife or some other weapon. He turns away and heads for the ger.

Maybe he's going to get help? Another possibility is him rallying support to lure me into the ger. He reappears with his wife and daughter in tow. They wear matching purple shirts. They'll help— yes, I'm sure they will. I remount and display the pony's antics, but they laugh when he hurls me up his neck. Help? I am merely the act of the day. I get off and walk the slumbering chestnut away.

It will take two hours to walk the last 7 kilometers. I turn back to the man shamelessly and point at the horse on his line. With striving eyebrows I ask him if I can ride it. It will cost me $20, he says, performing his fingers. An alarm sounds inside me. I cannot pay for a pony to taxi me to the finish.

Again the chestnut and I plod away up the hill together. I tickle his withers as I gaze into the air. Devan will be crossing the finish line. She is almighty. She is surely the winner. Has the Derby ever seen so fierce a competitor? I must remember to send her a card.

I am slightly embarrassed by the prospect of finishing second. Yet seven days ago I could barely imagine finishing.

With the competition lifted, I can feel the land more than ever. I notice the involuntary drone of all the small forms around me. Maybe things and people don't need to be convincing, they just need to exist. I find it hard to imagine what we've been doing riding from station to station all this time. In moments like this, I catch glimpses of myself uncertain, as though the only truth I can rely upon is human extinction.

> I strangely missed myself, who I imagine
> To be a living being either of ancient times or the
>   future

Ayurzana Gun-Aajav taps into my confusions about where I might even be, at any one time.

We've been walking side by side for about ten minutes when the noise of a motorbike engine expands from the land. I look up to see a machine blazing along the edge of the plain. It turns towards me. A man. Not another.

The figure draws in and gets off his motorbike. His arms hang gently from his shoulders. I recognize him as the gangly teenager from the last station who helped choose this horse. There's a quiet tension between us until he climbs onto the chestnut and kicks and whips with more might than I ever dared use. I see the horse walk forward, drudging out of his grump. The boy whips on and the chestnut trots a little. A miracle of force? A forced miracle?

I haven't a moment to question. We swap places. I kick, shout, and imagine action. The boy revs his motorbike up the pony's bottom to scare him onwards. We find the trot again. For half a kilometer, the boy revs, adding hoots for good measure. We trail over the steppe noisily. By the time he hands me back my helmet we are trotting well, but when he takes his motorbike away the pony stops again. He returns to push us onwards once more. Then he recedes into the emptiness, waving once.

Agreeably, truthfully, we antler our way towards the end. I ride with a free head, carrying my helmet in one hand and the pony's reins in the other. The strong line of mountains above us unpacks into bouldered outcrops. It's as though a giant has been playing Lego. One of these forms is the wishing rock, which the map book tells us to make a wish at. Passersby have paid their respects with blue scarves and empty bottles of Chinggis Khan vodka, but I have nothing left to wish for. Does it matter—will it ever—that I have faded, like the weather? That I will be second again?

"Wish" is a word from the magical world—originally the

wishing rod, or magic wand. To wish is not just to desire; it is a form of action.

I'd like to end here, in this eventful final leg—the refusing horse, the groping man, the apparitional boy. I belong in this chain of hiccups. I don't want to add any more—no words, no strides. But the finish is cantering towards me: I can see it now on the distant slope. I keep glancing away in the hope it will slide off the curve of the earth. I dread docking back into the human web.

Shall we press our paws on land? Do we dare?

The anthill grows into an array of vehicles and humans clustered around a flimsy flag. Closer, we reach Richard, who seems naked without his jeep. I'm ashamed to say I'm ashamed to look at him. He's on a different tack, snapping us from every angle, scuttling as though the ground is an electric current he can't touch for long. This is the most animated I've seen him all week.

"Put your helmet on," he says through a clenched jaw as we pass.

What's he on about?

"No, I can't be bothered."

"Devan's about to get a penalty. Put your bloomin' helmet on or you'll be disqualified."

The surprise stuns the land. I see it curling inwards.

I mean, in theory I can believe Devan has a heart rate penalty. She's been so close to incurring one all day. But not at this point, not with this significance—the possibility of losing her victory. It will relegate her two hours and I will eat balloons.

The chestnut shuffles the meter onwards. Richard sprints after us. Photo. Click. Further photos. Clickalicklick. My ears feel like two jokes protruding from my head. I don't like the urgency of his command but I throw myself over this obstacle and lay the helmet on my head with the floppiest of wrists. As the sweated nylon merges with my wet forehead, Richard dashes in front of us for the final seconds.

XXXIX

In my recurring Mongol Derby dreams, I never win. Often the race doesn't get to the end of itself at all. It's as though the finish isn't the point, nor even the direction in which the energy has been thrusting. There's rarely a sequence of one-after-another; time and space flex and vanish. Sometimes Devan is on fighting form, way ahead of the pack. Often Devan isn't there at all.

I holler at the chestnut as we scuttle towards the finishing stick, asking him to pick up some speed to protect us from the end. My tummy is stagnating. I'm scared Richard might be lying. And I'm also scared Richard might *not* be lying, which would turn my random August escapade into a miserably predictable story, equipped with a victorious underdog and everything. If they crown me winner, I'll be left stranded on the finish island, fumbling for excuses for my conformity.

We crumple to a standstill as soon as we pass the stick. Then the pixie within me bounds out to tell stories of the leg to the awaiting audience, like a traveling circus unpacking for a stay: the chestnut's resignation (his ears are cocked back, listening), the search for help, and the groping man.

"And then, I *slapped* him . . ."

My monologue prevents anyone from cushioning me in congratulations or serving up other compliments. I've never been able to take compliments and this has frustrated my aunt in the past, who has instructed me to accept them graciously. One of my difficulties with them is their pointedness. They stop me in space for assessment and solidify me into a singular human, an absolute *me* I am never quite sure of.

When I lay my voice down at the end of the report, I notice faces looking at me that are not blades of grass. These are humans— pulled-out riders and tired crew—and their looks suggest I might've missed the point. *What are you doing?* they seem to say.

It's glee! I scream from within, but cannot make noise. I look down at the crowd of silently giggling grass instead.

"Don't you know Devan's been given a penalty?" asks Georgie, stepping forward with her arms folded. She and her neighbor share a funereal expression, the same one I used to face when in deep trouble at school.

After sliding off the horse, I look about in search of Charles and his promised vodka. His absence bruises the scene, yet I'm more relaxed because of it. Maggie stands close by in her familiar empress stance. Behind her I see Devan's black horse—head low, body heaving, steam rising from his flanks, flies circling and licking his sweat.

◆

There I was in a formation of people, us all looking at one another. Was this what being human had been before the race, and would become again?

I wasn't in tune with the tension that had built up among those waiting. Maybe being on the move had kept me free of that kind of gravity. If meaning is linked to place, how can you keep hold of it when rivering along? Yet Devan had managed to weigh the race down in gravity from start camp onwards. Perhaps this was what upset me. I wanted to seize conceptual power back, contesting not just her victory but also whether the Derby mattered as much as she thought it did.

"This is not the blooming Olympics—it's a joke race," I said to Georgie, with whom I talked for a while after the crowd dispersed, mainly about her coccyx, which was nigh on broken and had forced her to pull out of the race.

On the twelfth minute, my chestnut's heart rate dropped and Maggie strode over.

"Lara?"

She handed me the prize. A blue can of beer.

"Congratulations. You are our winner."

The words traveled up my spine in spasms. We chinked cans and took a sip each. Approximately three people applauded. I passed my can on to someone who liked beer, all the while unsure how to proceed with myself. I held my lips straight and appeared unfazed, waving off the moments like a series of bad smells. There seemed little point in expressing my confused feelings when I could depend on them to pass. Shame lit up my cheeks. It was inconvenient to have accidentally—or, rather, fully intentionally—won the whole thing. Victory snatched away both my moral high horse and my anonymity. Already I'd become the object of mistrusting stares. I hadn't thought about how the person who wins the world's toughest horse race ought to act, let alone feel.

Why couldn't I just be triumphant, like an elephant squirting water? In other words, where was Devan when you needed her? Heaped on the ground apart from her pony, weeping with her head in her hands, unavailable for the outsourcing of my victory celebrations.

I felt an urge to become little, and crawl into the cave of my mother's long green coat, that snaily home of Mummy-dark, the age-old promise of "security." The chestnut pony grazed behind me, his mouth breaking the blades of grass as he moved around the care of his poised foreleg, the experience gone from his body already. Well, what was triumph, really?

Later, after we had disbanded, I would wonder why the moment could not contain me, or why I couldn't contain it, and also whether there was such a thing as being dignified without being ostentatious. It had seemed best to sacrifice both, and be embarrassed. I hadn't worked out that the idea of "one" winner made no sense to me, in the end. How could Devan not be included in the story anymore? It was almost as if victory itself became the villain, and the less I enjoyed it, the closer I came to annihilating it.

Devan was quaking like a washing machine. So long had she lived as a parasite in my mind that her real body had me shuddering with tenderness. At least she'd enjoyed thinking she'd won in the hour before the penalty. The crowd had clapped for her and the steward had let her ring home on the satellite phone to tell her dad the good news.

Maggie caught me looking at Devan and nudged me in her direction. I slunk over and curled my arms around her. She unfurled to embrace me back.

"I'm sorry," I said in the midst of our hug, not thinking of what I meant—it seemed my apologetic female mode had switched on.

No matter. Devan was crying and I assume she could barely hear me. My limp hug had to be enough. Perhaps it was now that we found the Everest spirit that had so eluded us during the race. All the emotion taking up the space between us dissolved—not because we were hung from a rope nearing death, but because the charade was over, and we were in touch. Devan raised her head and looked me in the eye for the first time since start camp. Her face shone red with sunburn; her lips were so chapped the peeling white skin appeared as a second set of teeth surrounding her smile.

"Congratulations," she said. Her American accent made it sound like gift wrap to my British ears.

I replied that what had happened wasn't fair, and added, "Just the way things work out. I guess we're both winners, really."

Her eyes fell. "Yeah," she said.

It turned out she did agree. Within a week, she would tell the American press that her final horse had the flu, and she was therefore the real winner of the race.

XL

The closure of a race so long came with no particular sensation. Finish camp was wedged below a high ridge, so my inner hamster at last had a corner to withdraw into. Nonetheless, it took time for me to slow down. Thirty-six hours after the Mongol Derby's end, I had the urge to go for a run, and liked the idea of asking Devan if I could borrow her running shoes. It would be as though nothing had happened—which really I wasn't sure it had. Winning disappeared in a few cow-munched moments. So, I hoped, had coming second.

From her sunstruck malady in the ger, which she seemed not to have left since the end of the race except to go to the toilet, Devan handed out her shoes, and in my bunions leapt. I ran off slightly out of balance—questioning, as ostriches must do on a daily basis, why I found myself on two legs instead of four.

It took three days for the rest of the riders to drift in. The doctor strode around camp topless, perfecting his crimson suntan.

I spent much of my time in a state of extreme laughter with the South African vets, Helen and Pete. We were achieving a level of pained hilarity I usually only reach with my mother.

I did not call home during this post-race period—after the conversation with family on the last leg, I sensed they might be terribly jubilant and profiting from what my father would no doubt be marketing as a "success." I later found out he had called the organizers and demanded to speak to his daughter. Although the family had been gripped by this curious race 8,000 kilometers away, they had only been eyeing my dot as it crawled around a screen—and there in cyberspace I remained at finish camp, a dot ungraspable. The idea of it pleases me to this day.

Mum, meanwhile, had—unknown to me—experienced a feverish sickness near the climax of the race and checked herself into hospital, something no one has ever known her to do. And when Devan was declared the winner on Twitter, everyone slumped back into their armchairs except Arthur, who scuttled up to his bedroom to await better news, strangely convinced I would somehow still win.

One week after the finish, as the plane lifted me out of Ulaanbaatar's steel palette, my stomach ached extra and I began to cry. It always seemed to happen like this—my strongest bout of emotion arriving well after the event, when I was suspended between two worlds.

I didn't like returning to England—not then, not ever—although something in me likes the grass there. My immediate family were not in the country when I arrived. I was collected from the airport by none other than Aunt Lucinda, who emerged from her hiding place in the earth's mantle to express her surprise. She returned me to Appleshaw, where unfettered blue tits perched in the bushes, watching us come, having seen us go.

And, like the baseless fabric of this vision,
The cloud-capp'd towers, the gorgeous palaces,
The solemn temples, the great globe itself,
Ye all which it inherit, shall dissolve.

I'm still amazed I took something so highbrow as *The Tempest*
in my backpack—without caring, without meaning it to mean
anything.

Sometimes a thousand twangling instruments
Will hum about mine ears, and sometimes voices
That, if I then had waked after long sleep,
Will make me sleep again: and then, in dreaming,
The clouds methought would open and show
   riches
Ready to drop upon me, that when I waked,
I cried to dream again.

This was Shakespeare's final play, a play of dream, spirit, and
sea. I like the way it sounds, feminine and free.

XLI

A woman at a dinner party tells me she died and came back to life. "I haven't felt the same since," she says across the wide wooden table. Then she wonders, "Did the Derby change you?"

Woah, I reply. I can't say it did. Seven days spent edging my way through land and air? Not really.

Well, maybe it endorsed a haphazard manner. Maybe in years to come, I will see it as a seal on the years that went before it.

I rain maybes.

The race did seem to lend me some faith in my placement in this world, and that faith released an energy my teenage sloth-self had let go of—I felt it fueling me for months afterwards. Anne Carson talks about the dilemma of the pilgrim who reaches her destination and "cannot bear to stop." It's true an idea of freedom has come to swamp my mind, taking me places I never fully intend to end up. One night I'll find myself cycling south out of Edinburgh with London in mind; the next month, a friend and I will end up boarding a thirty-two-hour bus from Istanbul to Iraq.

Maybe this restlessness is serving to keep some part of me alive. Or maybe I move to avoid making—making words, friends, and love. I do spread my heart thinly as I go. Will I ever accept that the most mythic, meaningful life might lie in the ordinary: the kingdom of details and daily reprises? For now, I'm stunned by all things static, scared by the idea that a "home" might exist for me somewhere.

Our human habit is to make endings of things—close them, wrap them up, slap a cap on unruly time. But what use is a conclusion or an understanding when all I want to do is open up, mess up, unpack, and unreel?

Endings fade, but the force behind a story lives on. It passes through lifetimes, daughter to daughter. This being human means inhabiting an unfinished form, forever moving on to the next thing.

Three years after the Derby, I travel to Somerset to see a witch doctor for my seven-year-old stomach aches. She knows nothing about me except my pain. For an hour she pops in and out of the room to touch my body and let it settle.

"You," she says, as I stand on the threshold of a winter night, "are a pack of racehorses, waiting for the gates to open."

Author's Note

This book follows the brief experience of a foreigner in Mongolia. If you would like to read further and deeper into Mongolia, there is some brilliant Mongolian literature available in translation.

I've especially enjoyed the work of Ölziitögs Luvsandorj, whose witty short story "Aquarium," translated by Sainbayar Gundsambuu and K. G. Hutchins, was published by *Words Without Borders* and can be found on that organization's website. Thirteen of Ölziitögs's poems, many drawing from city life, were translated by Sh Tsog and have been published on the *Best American Poetry* website in a series of posts by Simon Wickham-Smith titled "Modern Mongolian Literature in Seven Days." The series also features work by poets such as Ayurzana Gun-Ajaav and Mend-Ooyo Gombojav. *The End of the Dark Era*, a recent collection by the adventurous poet Tseveendorjin Oidov (translated by Simon Wickham-Smith), is the first book of Mongolian poetry to be published in the United States.

For more on steppe life, *The Blue Sky* is a stunning novel by Galsan Tschinag (translated from German by Katharina Rout) charting the daily rhythms of nomadic life. Byambasuren Davaa's 2005 film, *In the Cave of the Yellow Dog*, is now also a book coauthored with Lisa Reisch (translated into English by Sally-Ann Spencer).

In the English language, Uuganaa Ramsay's memoir, *Mongol*, shifts between Scotland, Ulaanbataar, and the steppe. *A Monastery in Time: The Making of Mongolian Buddhism*, by Caroline Humphrey and Hurelbaatar Ujeed, is an academic study of Mongolian Buddhism. *Time, Causality and Prophecy in the Mongolian Cultural Region*, edited by Rebecca Empson, is a fascinating collection of essays by a range of authors.

Acknowledgments

Letters of deep gratitude keep forming in my head—

To Robyn Drury and Jonathan Lee: I'm a cavorting-snorting foal at having been edited by the both of you.

To Zoe Ross, who landed *Rough Magic* the loveliest homes:
    Catapult—thanks to Andy Hunter, Pat Strachan, Jennifer Abel Kovitz, Megan Fishmann, Lena Moses-Schmitt, Wah-Ming Chang, and everyone on the wondrous team.
    Ebury—thanks to everyone, especially Sarah Bennie and her team.

To Josephine Rowe, for appreciating each pony and leading them to Jonathan.

To Brittany Newell, for being provocative.

To Parwana Fayyaz, Jamie Helyar, and Sadhana Senthilkumar for inspiration and affection.

To Eavan Boland, John Evans, and Tobias Wolff for new beginnings; and to Dana Kletter ("you can be self-deprecating and British all day long but at some point you've got to hit hard and say something real").

To Aishwary Kumar, for teachings unfathomable.

To Harriet Clark, Shatra Galbadrah, Sue Mott, Katy Willings, and, depthlessly, to Neal Gething.

To each sister and brother who read this through and offered advice.

To anyone who let me be lonely, and to those who did not.

To so many of the above for their attentiveness, often from afar, when I've been unwell. To my doctors of all kinds.

To those who homed me beyond their call—the Dorset boghills and their Hugheses, Kildale and her Sutcliffes, Anita George-Carey on the river, the Chalabys all over, and the Alegrias & animals in California. You have each allowed me to write in a place where places can exist.

To all the nonhuman forces, especially horses, Appleshaw, the Pacific, the steppe, the Plains and elsewhere, for their care.

© Richard Dunwoody

LARA PRIOR-PALMER was born in London in 1994. She studied conceptual history and Persian at Stanford University. In 2013, she competed in the 1,000-kilometer Mongol Derby in Mongolia, sometimes described as the world's toughest and longest horse race, and became the first woman to win the race, and the youngest person ever to finish. *Rough Magic* is her first book.